Tiffany,

Trust God no matter what!

Love,
Natalie
5/17/15

Stormy Weather

Twenty-Five Lessons Learned while
Weathering the Storms of Life

Natalie Brown Rudd

WESTBOW·
PRESS
A DIVISION OF THOMAS NELSON
& ZONDERVAN

WestBow Press books may be ordered through booksellers or by contacting:

WestBow Press
A Division of Thomas Nelson & Zondervan
1663 Liberty Drive
Bloomington, IN 47403
www.westbowpress.com
1 (866) 928-1240

Because of the dynamic nature of the Internet, any web addresses or links contained in
this book may have changed since publication and may no longer be valid. The views
expressed in this work are solely those of the author and do not necessarily reflect the
views of the publisher, and the publisher hereby disclaims any responsibility for them.

Any people depicted in stock imagery provided by Thinkstock are models,
and such images are being used for illustrative purposes only.
Certain stock imagery © Thinkstock.

ISBN: 978-1-4908-6851-6 (sc)
ISBN: 978-1-4908-6853-0 (hc)
ISBN: 978-1-4908-6852-3 (e)

Library of Congress Control Number: 2015901577

Printed in the United States of America.

WestBow Press rev. date: 02/04/2015

This book is dedicated to my dad, the late Minister Elijah Brown Jr. and my mom, Gwendolyn Brown, for laying the foundation of Jesus Christ in my life and to my daughter, Alexis for teaching me to keep dancing in the midst of the storms.

Contents

Foreword

I'm sure there have been times in your life when you've felt like there were more rainy days than sunny days and that you didn't know how you were going to make it through without drowning. However, it's important to know and recognize the difference between a rainy day and an actual storm. A storm is defined in *Webster's Dictionary* as "a serious disturbance of an element of nature." Sometimes, certain elements in your life present serious disturbances: Your mortgage is being foreclosed, you've been downsized and are too old to get another job, you have medical insurance but can't afford the co-pay, you are working full time and taking care of an elderly family member (or members), someone in your family has a long-term illness … the list can go on and on.

It's inevitable that we all go through storms. It's how we handle the storm that's important. Do you question why God allowed the storm in your life? Do you become angry with God and others around you, or do you recognize each storm as an opportunity to praise God? If you truly want to see the storms of your life in a different way, if you want to look at them through the eyes of God, and if you want to learn how to handle them, then this book is for you!

I've known Natalie Brown Rudd since she was teenager, and it has been a joy to watch her grow and mature into adulthood. Yet it was in my Bible study class that I really got to know her well and observe her love for the Lord and for His Word, and to see His wisdom blossom and grow in her. I saw her accept the call to the preaching ministry, and I was blessed to see her go through her storms. I witnessed firsthand how she handled the challenges and emerged a more trusting, confident, and faithful Christian. As you read this book, you will witness a personal testimony of how a child of God should, and can, handle the storms of life.

If you are currently experiencing a storm, then the way Natalie tells the story of her "right-now" storm experience is enough to encourage you to say, "If God did this for Natalie, then He will certainly do it for me, too." Natalie's writings also show those of you who are approaching a storm how to get through it, where to direct your focus, and how to recognize that there is a purpose for your storm.

For those of you who are coming out of a life storm, this book can be a measuring stick to show you how much of your life you have really given to the Lord. Do you still trust God and give Him praise? Have you come out of your storm a changed person? When you finish reading, no matter where you are in the storm journey of your life, you will realize that you can face any of life's storms because you *know* that God is in control. You *know* that He has a purpose for your particular storm, and you *know* that your trust is always safely placed in Him and Him alone!

Deacon Delores Brown
Relationships Director
Antioch Baptist Church
Cleveland, Ohio

Introduction

These things I have spoken unto you, that in Me ye
might have peace. In the world ye shall have tribulation:
but be of good cheer; I have overcome the world.
(John 16:33 KJV)

It's 1:00 a.m. on July 11, 2012. I have to go to the bathroom, but, as I move around in bed, I realize that I have a tiny pinch of chest pain. Now I question myself: Did I wake up because I have to go to the bathroom or because I have chest pain? Hmm … but the pain is so tiny. Is it real?

As I walk to the bathroom, I don't notice any other problems. I think to myself, *I must be imagining it.*

I walk back to the bedroom and sit on the edge of the bed to assess if the pain is still there. Yes, it is there—the size of the tip of my index finger.

I ask the Lord what I should do and to please make it clear, no time to second-guess. Do I go back to bed, or do I call 9-1-1?

As I lie back down in the bed, the pain becomes more widespread. It travels up my neck, across my chest, and to my left shoulder.

It is clear now: Call 9-1-1.

Several hours later, I was at the emergency room. The ER doctor said I had a condition called pleurisy, an inflammation around the lungs that can cause chest pain. I said to myself, *Pleurisy? No way! How? Clearly, he doesn't know what he is talking about.*

Out loud, I said, "Doctor, are you sure it is pleurisy?"

"Any tuberculosis?" he asked.

"No, sir," I replied.

"Have you had any recent trauma to your chest, congestive heart failure, or a collapsed lung?"

"No, sir, I have not," I replied sternly so he could sense my impatience.

"Then it must be related to an upper-respiratory infection or a virus," he said.

"I don't have any upper-respiratory signs or symptoms," I said. "I felt fine when I went to bed."

"I'm not sure, but it will clear up in a few days," he assured me. "Just take the steroids and get some rest." After making that statement, he quickly walked out of the room and moved onto his next patient.

I went home confused and in pain, baffled by what was happening. It just didn't make any sense to me.

From that point on, my days became focused on controlling my pain. My sole priority was to find a comfortable position in bed and not to move for as long as possible. I told my family to kindly wake me when the storm was past and the pain was gone.

That didn't happen.

This particular storm is what I call my "health crisis." My life has changed completely because of an unexpected health problem that causes extreme debilitating pain—pain that should go away but that, for some reason, has not, making me feel like I am losing my mind. Have you ever felt that way? One day, I was feeling great. The next day, I awoke in pain that seemed to have come out of nowhere. The pain causes sleeplessness and long, tearful nights, redirecting my normal routine into doctor appointments, multiple trips to the pharmacy, and countless tests and treatments, yet resulting in no relief from whatever this condition is, no clear answers to my questions, and no end in sight. If I am honest, then I have to say that this storm has shaken my entire world.

So many nights (and days) I spend crying out to God and asking for a healing. It has been quite a while, and the healing hasn't quite come as I wanted. This has been the most physically painful experience I have ever encountered. Day in and day out, the pain is there. I wake up with it and go to bed with it.

I have learned that storms can turn one's life upside down. As from the moment I awoke with this pain, everything I do is centered on my pain, and nothing else matters. I haven't had the energy or physical strength to go to work, go grocery shopping, pay bills, or do any of the things necessary to function.

Thank goodness that I am blessed with a family and a retired mother who can be here every day, tending to whatever is needed. When you are not feeling well, no matter how old you are, there is nothing like a mother's love. She knows what you need before you do, and there's no need to ask, because she is always a step ahead, doing what is needed.

My friend, life has so many twists and turns that take us by surprise. Yet we serve a God who is never thrown off by what we experience in life. I have learned that lesson on more than one occasion, but somehow, with each new experience, I initially forget. Thankfully, God keeps reminding me. Every morning, I wake up having survived another night of pain. I thank the Lord for sending me His healing. Even though the healing is not complete, meaning that the pain is not gone completely, I am getting better each day.

Thank God for Jesus and the Holy Spirit. If it were not for Them, I have no idea where I would be! Do you hear me?

Can you relate?

There is an awesome passage of Scripture, Isaiah 43:2, that can comfort you when you find yourself in a storm. Read the words slowly and allow them to marinate your spirit. The words are from God through the prophet Isaiah to the Israelites while they were being held in captivity. "When you pass through the waters, I will be with you; and when you pass through the rivers, they will not sweep over you. When you walk through the fire, you will not be burned; the flames will not set you ablaze" (NIV).

Did you read the words God spoke to His people?

Did you allow them to marinate?

No matter what situation you are facing, no matter where you find yourself at this moment, take comfort in the reassurance that you will not be overcome by this storm. Most important, remember that God says He will be with you. What an awesome promise from God, who is faithful to His Word! He is saying that no matter what the storm is made of, you will not be overcome by it! That is worth shouting about! And then He goes on to say that He is with you! Hallelujah! God is with you and with me when the storms of life are raging all around us. We can be of good cheer, because Jesus says that He has already taken care of it *all!* My cousin Sonya said it like this: "It's already all right!"

If you are anything like me, then you will need to memorize this verse, write it down on Post-it Notes all around your house, and mark it with a highlighter in your Bible, just to remind yourself that this storm will not overcome you and you will awake to another day of sunshine, for this storm will not last forever.

Trust in God, your loving Father, and know that better days are ahead.

Now, before we go any further ...

Have you accepted Jesus Christ as your Savior? Have you confessed your sins and received the Holy Spirit in your heart? It is essential that you are standing on a solid foundation if you are truly to be able to weather the storms of life. Every lesson that I have learned and will discuss in the following pages is based on my relationship with God the Father, Jesus the Son, and the Holy Spirit. Can you weather the storms without being a believer of Jesus Christ? Absolutely, but this book will not make sense to you if you are not.

If you have not received Christ in your heart, then you can take the time right now to do this by praying the following prayer:

> Heavenly Father, have mercy on me, a sinner. I believe in You and that Your word is true. I believe that Jesus Christ is the Son of the living God and that He died on the cross so that I may now have forgiveness for my sins and eternal life. I know that without You in my heart, my life is meaningless. I believe in my heart that You, Lord God, raised Him from the dead. Please, Jesus, forgive me for every sin

I have ever committed or done in my heart. Please, Lord Jesus, forgive me and come into my heart as my personal Lord and Savior today. I need You to be my Father and my friend. I give You my life and ask You to take full control from this moment on; I pray this in the name of Jesus Christ. Amen.

Once you have prayed this prayer, believe in your heart that you are a child of God. You are one of His children, and you have received the gift of the Holy Spirit within you.

Welcome to the family!

Now, let's continue reading.

How to Use this Book

This book initially started off as a journal during the storm of my health crisis. I often use journaling to pray and release any feelings I am experiencing at a given time. I find it amazing to read back through what I've written and see how I felt at that moment and how God answered my prayers. So, this book was literally birthed out of the storm that attacked my body with intense pain and overwhelming exhaustion. My life was completely turned upside down. It is only by the grace of God that I was able to capture this moment on paper.

Many nights I spent crying out in pain and praying for relief and comfort. During those moments, I was unable to recall any Scripture to help ease my mind and calm my fears. My mind was so overwhelmed by pain that I could not find any relief. One way I was able to combat the long, painful nights was to enter into praise and worship. When I found myself in a low, dark, and lonely place, unable to recall the Scriptures, I found comfort in listening to the lyrics of Christian music. The words flooded my head, took me to a place of praising God in the midst of my tears, and soothed my aching soul. When I couldn't remember the Scriptures, the lyrics reminded me of His promises and of His faithfulness in the good times and the bad.

Never before have I been blessed by music like I have in this storm. It became a nighttime ritual for me to place my Nook or iPad under my pillow, click on the Pandora app, and select a Nicole C. Mullen,

CeCe Winans, or Casting Crowns station and allow the lyrics to whatever song came on to literally pour into my head. As my tears fell, I found myself singing and praising God. It would soothe my aching body, ease my mind, calm my heart, and literally distract me from my pain and anxious thoughts.

There are three key points to every lesson discussed in this book: a Bible scripture, a prayer, and a song. Use all three to help you embrace the lesson. Use the Bible Scripture as part of your devotion for the day. Study and memorize it. If it is particularly helpful to you, then write it down on a small card and carry it with you. Refer to it throughout your day to remind you of God's Word, His promises to you.

The prayer at the end of each section is to be used to jump-start your own prayer. Take this time to talk to your Father, who is always there waiting for you to approach His throne of grace to obtain all that you need to weather the storms of life. Go to Him in prayer, pouring out whatever you are experiencing, whatever is causing you anxiety or overwhelming your heart. God already knows, and He cares about you.

The song at the end of each section can be listened to on YouTube. I would suggest watching a video that has the lyrics available to review. Allow the song to create an atmosphere of worship and praise while you pray. Nothing takes the place of Scripture, especially when we are in a storm, but music can be a wonderful blessing that ushers us into the presence of God. Please do not get caught up in whether you like the song, whether you like the artist's performance, or whether you like or dislike the music. Instead, get caught up in the lyrics, which will lead you to praise and worship. It's all about the lyrics' soothing your mind and your heart.

My hope and prayer for this book is to share with you what I l have learned through this and the other storms of my life. I pray that you will be able to use this book as a guide to help you navigate through whatever storm you are experiencing. I believe that our experiences are to be used to share with others along this journey. I pray that the lessons I have learned will help you and that, in turn, you will pass the lesson on to others.

Be forever blessed.

In this you greatly rejoice, though now for a little while you may have had to suffer grief in all kinds of trials. These have come so that your faith—of greater worth than gold, which perishes even though refined by fire—may be proved genuine and may result in praise, glory and honor when Jesus Christ is revealed.

(1 Peter 1:6–7 NIV)

Lesson 1

Storms Turn One's Life Upside Down

Do not boast about tomorrow, for you do
not know what a day may bring.
(Proverbs 27:1 NIV)

Yesterday's forecast was for sunny, warm weather. It is comfortable and not too humid—the perfect weather to be outdoors.

Today's forecast includes storm clouds, rain with treacherous winds, and flood warnings in certain areas.

That is the reality of life. One day, you are feeling fine, enjoying the warm, beautiful weather. The next day, you wake up and find that life as you know it has changed. The change may be permanent or just for a season. It is really too hard to tell in the very beginning. Every appointment on your calendar—canceled. Every errand on your never-ending to-do list goes undone. You call off from work— and who cares about breakfast? You just lost your appetite.

Where are you, and what has happened to your life?

My friend, you are in a storm.

The storms of life come unannounced and without warning. They have a way of changing our priorities and routines. Just as a tornado destroys everything in its path, a life storm can turn a person's life completely upside down.

But there is good news! The Bible tells us that while in this life we will have trials and tribulations, we should "be of good cheer," as Jesus has overcome them all (John 16:33).

Not some, but *all*.

How reassuring to know that when the storms of life are raging all around us, Jesus has overcome them all!

- ✓ Storms that threaten our health—Jesus has got it.
- ✓ Storms that empty our checking, savings, and retirement accounts—He's got that, too.
- ✓ Storms that steal our mental health and peace of mind—check.

Relationship storms, children storms, job storms—as with any type of storm you face in this life, Jesus says, "I have overcome them all."

Yet we still have to endure the storms, as no one is exempt from experiencing them. It reminds me of the old saying that you are either in trouble, walking out of trouble, or on your way to trouble. Let's face it: It is a natural part of life that trouble will head your way, threatening everything you hold dear—your health, your family, your job, your material comforts, and, most of all, your peace of mind.

As Christians, we can find comfort in the words, "God is our refuge and our strength, an ever-present help in trouble" (Psalm 46:1). There isn't any storm, trouble, or situation we face in life that God cannot handle. And, in the midst of stormy weather, He can restore our peace of mind when we keep our minds on Him, in spite of what is going on around us.

May I be transparent with you for a second? I still get overwhelmed and want to run in the opposite direction when I find myself in stormy weather. Can you relate?

Even though we have this reassurance, we must say, if we are honest, that our hearts and minds still become overwhelmed and filled with anxiety. We question ourselves and anyone who will listen. "How can I endure storms that turn my life upside down? How can I continue moving forward when I am flat on the ground with worry and fear?"

We find ourselves asking questions like, "Why is this happening?" "When will it end?" "What are we supposed to do in the meantime while waiting for this storm to pass?" "Do I stop trusting God and start doubting His love for me because I am in a storm? Or do I cling even tighter to my faith in Him?"

These are questions I found in my heart every day at the beginning of my storm. All of them are valid questions, but not all are relevant or beneficial. You see, I learned a long time ago that God typically does not answer the "why" questions. I believe they go unanswered because God does not owe us an explanation for anything that happens in our lives. I know this is a tough pill to swallow, yet it is the reality. Ask Job. Did God show up and answer any of his "why" questions? What about Jesus? While dying on the cross, He called out to God and asked, "Why have you forsaken me" (Matthew 27:46b)? He received no response. God doesn't seem to be interested in answering our "why" questions.

So, we find ourselves struggling with not understanding why life isn't going the way we would like or how we planned. However, would knowing why this was happening stop it from happening? Would knowing why change any of our circumstances? The answer would be a resounding *no.* Knowing the reasons behind the storm doesn't take the storm away.

I am learning that the most important question we can focus on, one that will benefit us in the midst of this storm, is very simple: What do we do when we awake to stormy weather?

What do we do when life as we know it has changed and everything is beyond our control? What do we do while we wait for this storm to pass over? What do we do when life has turned upside down?

This has been my focus since I stopped fighting the storm I am currently experiencing. I have poured my heart out in prayer, asking the Lord to show me how to weather this storm that threatens my health and seems to be ruining my quality of life. How do I persevere when my body is awash with pain and I am homebound? I have found myself screaming, "Lord, how do I deal with these unwanted changes that I cannot control?"

Day after day, these were the questions that filled my heart and burdened my mind from the time I awoke until I went to sleep. "Lord, what do I do in stormy weather?"

The message was simple, and I want to share it with you.

Get to know God while waiting. Draw closer to His presence. Let go, and start to trust His ways. Lean into the everlasting arms of our Savior. This is what we do while we wait. It is deeper than I ever imagined.

Even when the storms of life are raging all around and life has turned upside down, I believe in God when He says, "I am your rock, your refuge, and your strength, and I have not moved." We have to learn to trust in God when the sun is shining beautifully *and* when the thunderstorms are raging all around.

Prayer

Gracious heavenly Father, thank You for being an all-seeing, all-knowing, and all-powerful God. This storm has come by surprise to me, but not to You. Even though I can't see my way past this moment, I will trust in Your ways and Your provision. Life as I know it has turned upside down, but I am thankful that You have not changed and that You are still God, no matter where I find myself today. Please continue to walk beside me, guiding me through this stormy weather. In Jesus' name, I pray. Amen.

Meditation Song

Meditate on the lyrics to the song "Let Go" by DeWayne Woods.

Lesson 2

Storms Are Holy Ground

"Do not come any closer," God said.
"Take off your sandals, for the place where
you are standing is holy ground."
(Exodus 3:5 NIV)

For a moment, I want you to recall the miraculous story of the transfiguration of Jesus as it is told in the Gospel of Luke, 9:28–35. In the story, Jesus took His disciples Peter, James, and John with Him up a mountain to pray. The Scripture tells us that while Jesus was praying, the appearance of His face changed and His clothes became as bright as a flash of lightning (verse 29). Then, Moses and Elijah appeared, talking with Jesus.

The disciples, who had fallen asleep, awoke to witness not only Jesus' glory but also the conversation with Moses and Elijah. Peter, who was awestruck, wanted to capture the moment and suggested to Jesus that they put up three shelters—one for Jesus, one for Moses, and one for Elijah. Before Jesus responded to Peter, a cloud appeared and wrapped around the three. A voice from the cloud said, "This is my Son, whom I have chosen; listen to Him" (verse 35).

Wow! Can you imagine if you witnessed Jesus transform into all of His glory in the presence of Moses and Elijah up on the mountain? Clearly, I would be like Peter, saying, "This is awesome! Can you believe what we are seeing?"

I think I can relate to Peter the best out of all of the disciples because he was real with others. He was the one who said and did what everyone else was thinking but was too afraid to say or do. He never tried to be politically correct; whatever was on his mind, he said.

This was an amazing moment for these disciples. Jesus lifted the veil of His glory and allowed the disciples a peek into His divinity. Why these three? I don't have a clue, but what an awesome privilege to be up on that mountain with Jesus and to hear the voice of God.

Clearly, this was a holy experience. And that is the point I want to make.

Up on this mountain, away from everyday life, right before their eyes, the disciples were part of something holy. They witnessed Jesus in all of His glory like no one else would before His death. And if that were not enough, God Himself spoke from a cloud, confirming that Jesus was indeed His Son and that the disciples were to listen to Him.

Absolutely amazing! Not only were these disciples part of a holy experience, but they also found themselves on holy ground. And I believe that we find ourselves on holy ground as well when we enter into a storm.

Now, I am sure that you are thinking that this storm you are experiencing is far from being holy and that I have totally lost my mind. But before you put this book down and tell everybody that I am crazy, please bear with me as I explain.

I believe that Jesus took the three disciples with Him up the mountain for several reasons, two which are relevant to the storms of life that we face today.

1. **He wanted to reveal His glory to the disciples.** If the disciples had any doubts that He was the Messiah, then Jesus revealing His glory would clear everything up. There would be no more room for doubt or questions. The fact that Moses and Elijah were there with Him confirmed that He was fulfilling both the Old Testament law (of Moses) and the teachings of the prophets (in this case, Elijah). You see, revealing His glory would change the disciples' view of Him from that point on. It would be impossible for them to witness His transfiguration and think the same about Him.

2. **He wanted the disciples to get to know Him better.** You see, to truly know God, you have to experience Him, not just read about Him in the Bible or hear a sermon about Him. You must actually *experience* Him on a personal and intimate level. Sometimes, the best way and place to get to know God is one-on-one up on a mountaintop. Mountaintop experiences are not just for successful moments; they are also a time when God takes you away from all that is familiar so you get to know Him better. Mountaintop experiences raise your level of understanding higher than you can imagine.

Whatever storm you are facing, know that God has removed you from your regular routine to go up on a mountain, where it is just the two of you. Even though you may feel that you are in the valley of darkness, God is saying, "Let me reveal some new attributes about

Myself to you that you can't understand while in your regularly too-busy, chaotic routine." Up on the mountain, God is guaranteed to have your full attention.

This Storm Is Your Holy Ground

You see, holy ground is where change happens. Holy ground is where God reveals Himself to us in new ways, ways that we cannot even imagine when we are flowing through our daily routines, going through life as usual. Because God knows us so well, He knows what is required to get our attention. Taking us up on the mountain is required when He wants to make major changes in our lives. He takes us up on the mountain to show us His splendor and all of His glory, and to reassure us that He is God and the *One* in control of our lives.

Recognize that this storm is a precious moment allowed by God for your own spiritual growth and maturity. I love how Charles Stanley said it in one of his *InTouch* publications:

> When adversity hits you like a ton of bricks, it could easily throw you into a pit of discouragement and despair. Although you may consider difficulties as setbacks, the Lord sees them as times for great advancement. His purpose for allowing them is not to destroy you but to stimulate your spiritual growth.[1]

I hope you didn't miss that last sentence—not to destroy us but to stimulate our spiritual growth.

This confirms that nothing happens in our lives that God doesn't use for our growth. Everything has meaning, and everything has a purpose. Oftentimes, we miss the meaning because of our limited, often tainted vision. We want things our way all of the time. But to

God who sees all, everything matters. I know now that these storms that we experience have a deeper message embedded within them. And if we become distracted or consumed by whatever is causing the storm, then we will miss what God is trying to say to us. We will also miss our blessing.

We are on holy ground.

Change is happening at this very moment.

God specifically designed this problem to get our attention so as to speak directly to our lives. Psalm 139:1–4 says that God knows every detail of our lives, He knows the words we will speak before we speak them; He knows our innermost feelings that we wrestle with. And because He knows us, He knows what storms will get our attention and speak directly to our hearts.

Now, I want you to understand one thing about this idea of being on holy ground. The Father of Lies, the Enemy of our souls, does not want us to look at storms as holy ground. No, his plan is for you to be so consumed with the problem and the pain that it causes you that you have no energy to be interested in anything else. He wants you to continue grumbling and complaining that life has turned upside down. He wants you to doubt God's love for you and focus on all that is wrong at this moment.

You see, if you are approaching this storm with all of the negative energy you can muster, if you are fighting it, cursing at it, then guess what? You will miss the blessings, the lessons you need to embrace. More important, you will miss getting to know God. And that is just where the Enemy wants you and me.

In the beginning of my storm, I spent several weeks caught up in my own pity party and missing God's voice, which was speaking through the clouds and rain. I was caught up in all that was wrong and was feeling sorry for myself. I think this is a normal human reaction. But I praise God that I didn't stay there and miss my blessing. I praise God because "greater is He that is within me than he that is in the world" (1 John 4:4) and because the Enemy has no authority over our lives. So, even though the Devil has a plan for us in this storm, so does God—and what the Enemy means for harm, God means for good.

In order to embrace the thought that the storms of life are holy ground, we have to see adversity through God's eyes and remember that everything He allows is for our benefit and for us to get to know Him better. It is actually a very precious moment meant for our good.

Prayer

Lord, help me in the midst of this storm to see my problems and my challenges through Your eyes. Help me to remember Your great love for me, and help me know that everything that happens in my life is because You allow it. I believe that You are allowing this storm to draw me closer unto You. Lord, I will be honest: I can barely see my way through the rain and clouds, but I am holding on to You. I am going to walk through this storm by faith and not by sight, trusting that all things will work according to Your good and perfect plan for my life. In Jesus' name, I pray. Amen.

Meditation Song

Meditate on the lyrics to the song "God Is Here" by Martha Munizzi.

Lesson 3

Storms Change Your Focus

And the peace of God, which transcends
all understanding, will guard your
hearts and minds in Christ Jesus.
(Philippians 4:7 NIV)

I am frequently telling my fourteen-year-old daughter to check her attitude. If you have ever been around teenagers or remember how you were at that age, then you understand exactly what I am saying.

And to tell the truth, we have to make the same type of attitude adjustment, especially when we find ourselves in the midst of a storm. We literally have to take a step back from our circumstances and check our attitude. We have to ask ourselves what has been our focus and how we have been responding to the storm.

I learned the hard way (because I am hardheaded!) to stop seeking answers to questions that didn't matter, like, "Why is this happening, and when will it be over?"

The Holy Spirit clearly said that the answers were not coming and that it would be in my best interests to change my focus. I received confirmation of that message one day while reading *Facing Illness with*

Hope, a wonderful book that my friend Saundra sent me. The author wrote, "Stay as concerned about the health of your faith as you are about the health of your body."[2]

In other words, all the time and energy I was spending on trying to figure out my health problems, I could have been spending reading the Word of God and getting to know Him better. It hit me like a ton of bricks that I had wasted so much time focusing on the wrong things.

Wow, the Enemy had me distracted, but only for that moment—and not one moment longer.

I realized that even though life had changed, God had not—for He is my rock that never moves. My "aha" moment came when I started to change my view of this storm, seeing it less as being a major inconvenience and more as taking place on holy ground. I learned to stop focusing on my problems and to start focusing on God's promises.

And then, of course, the test came to see if my focus had really changed.

Shortly after my "aha" moment, in the middle of the night, I found myself once again alone in pain, crying out to God. At that moment, the Holy Spirit told me to stop asking questions and just to ask for peace. All of a sudden, a spirit of peace washed over my mind and my body, calming my anxious heart. Finally, I was able to rest. That confirmed that this storm was my holy ground and that God was there in the midst of it, hearing my prayers and ministering to my needs.

As I shifted my focus, my questions changed from "why" to "what."

- What is it that You are saying to me?
- What is it that You want me to learn about You and about myself?

- What is it that I need to change?
- Is there something I need to let go of?
- What is it that I need to embrace?
- What is it that I need to read in Your Word?

I first prayed for forgiveness for my attitude and for the way I was responding to my situation. Then, I prayed that the Lord would soften my heart, refocus my lenses, and show me whatever it was that I needed to learn.

When I got to this place of wanting not miss to the lesson, my ears perked up and my antennae went up. I was on alert, determined not to miss God's message. He had me captivated by His mighty works. I knew that He had changed our relationship, and I was excited about what He was going to do.

Whatever the reason for our storm, God is there with us in the midst of it. We have to embrace the fact that God's plan is perfect, even if is difficult to understand and accept. We must submit to God's sovereignty because, no matter what, He will have His way. In other words, if the storm is here because we live in a fallen world, then God will have His way. If the storm is here from our doing, then God will have His way. If the storm is here because of a satanic attack, then guess what? God will still have His way.

Nothing will throw God off His game plan, and nothing catches God off guard. His perfect plan will be accomplished.

Keeping our minds on Christ will give us a peace that surpasses all understanding and help us weather this storm and those that come in the future. It is true that when we are approaching things we don't like, our attitude makes all the difference in the world.

Prayer

Merciful Father, I thank You for Your patience in dealing with me. Thank You for convicting me of my wrong attitude and giving me the desire to change. Lord, bless me now as I rely on the Holy Spirit to allow me to focus on drawing closer to You. I know that all of Your ways are good and faithful and that there are lessons that I need to learn in order to grow more like You. I will take this time to read Your Word, to meditate in Your presence, and to listen for Your still, small voice. Father, I thank You for this opportunity to walk closer with You. In Jesus' name, I pray. Amen.

Meditation Song

Meditate on the lyrics to the song "Who Am I" by Casting Crowns.

Lesson 4

Storms Are for a Far Greater Purpose

> In this you greatly rejoice, though now for a little
> while you may have had to suffer grief in all kinds of
> trials. These have come so that your faith—of greater
> worth than gold, which perishes even though refined
> by fire—may be proved genuine and may result in
> praise, glory and honor when Jesus Christ is revealed.
> (1 Peter 1:6–7 NIV)

I have subscriptions to several magazines that come to my house month after month. I never read them.

I always have the best intentions of reading them under the dryer at the hair salon, but I fall asleep the minute I sit down, or I am so engaged by the conversation with my fellow sisters that I forget all about the magazines in my bag. So, instead, I place them in a nice neat pile under the table in my home office, looking forward to the day when I can leisurely read them one by one.

Well, it turns out that here in this storm, I seem to have just that time.

And what a blessing—not the fact that I have time to read, but the lessons that I learned!

While resting one day (my new norm), my eye caught a fall edition of the magazine *Just Between Us.* If you have never heard of it, please check it out, as it is one of the best publications for Christian women. Now, mind you, this magazine had been sitting under my table for several weeks, yet I never once opened it, not even to browse for something that might be of interest to me.

Before I continue, I have to confess that, for some odd reason I cannot explain, I read magazines backward. I have no idea why I do this or where this weird habit came from, but it is what I do. The last article in this issue was titled "Fruitful in Affliction," by Shelly Esser. The article is about being fruitful when you are afflicted by pain, and it discusses how to stay faithful to God when you are facing challenges in your life. It seemed that every word was speaking to my situation, although the author and I didn't even know each other. How could she know what I was experiencing?

I was completely blown away!

Needless to say, my ears perked up and I sat straight up on my sofa, determined more than ever to read this entire magazine. Story after story dealt with challenges in life and accepting God's will.

As I was flipping through the magazine and devouring every article, I came across a very short section written by Shana Schutte titled "Doubt: A Catalyst to Faith?" Schutte used a quote from the book *The Gift of Doubt,* by Gary Parker, one that I think brings home the point about the storms of life having a greater purpose: "If faith never encounters doubt, if truth never struggles with error, if good never battles with evil, how can faith know its own power?"[3]

When I first read the quote, the words leaped off the page and came to life for me. If I ever needed to read this magazine, then the time was now, during this storm. It confirmed for me that our sovereign God knows that we grow through our adversity. It is through the storms of life that our faith is tested and we are drawn closer to God. And this is all for a far greater purpose than we can ever imagine. It reminds me of the Scripture on the fruit of the Spirit in Galatians 5:22: "But the fruit of the Spirit is love, joy, peace, patience, kindness, goodness, faithfulness, gentleness and self-control" (NIV).

These attributes are developed only through the storms of life. God, in all of His wisdom, knows this, and that is why, I believe, He allows these challenges to come in and turn our lives upside down. Flowers that withstand the storm grow and blossom into beautiful, fragrant bouquets. The key is that they don't wither and die in the storm. Instead, they are nourished by it and their roots grew deeper, which allows them to blossom.

The same is true with us: We blossom through our adversities.

In storms, our roots in Jesus grow deeper when we cling to Him and when we sit at His feet to get to know Him better. Everything God allows in our lives is for a far greater purpose than we can ever imagine or begin to comprehend. God wants our whole heart, and He will do whatever it takes to mold us into a vessel bearing His likeness, one that can be used for His glory.

Even though we don't like storms, they have the potential to produce a deeper understanding of God and allow us to become what He created us to be, which is more than conquerors glorifying Him.

Prayer

Lord, help me to accept Your will for my life. This storm I am experiencing makes me feel weary at times. I am struggling with clinging to You and seeing my way through all of the pain and heartache. I know that I need to trust in Your Word and not in my feelings. Help me, Holy Spirit, to rely on Your strength and power within myself. Help me to accept that this storm is for a far greater purpose than I can understand and to trust in God, no matter how I feel at this moment. In Jesus' name, I pray. Amen.

Meditation Song

Meditate on the lyrics to the song "Potter's Hand" by Chonda Pierce.

Lesson 5

We Run from Pain

Be still and know that I am God."
(Psalm 46:10 NIV)

In 1996, the popular movie *Twister* was released, starring Helen Hunt and Bill Paxton, who portrayed two scientists whose job was chasing tornados in order to perform an experiment in which they would capture data to predict future storms. When the weather forecast called for stormy weather, they went chasing after the storm rather than running in the opposite direction.

In reality, most of us run the other way when we see a storm coming.

But if storms are a natural part of life that serve a divine purpose, if they have meaning and come with lessons that cannot be learned in sunny weather, then why do we run from them? Why? Because, unlike the movie characters, it is in our DNA to run toward pleasure and away from anything that will cause us pain. It is a guarantee that no matter the source of your storm, you will experience some pain. It may come in the form of heartache from disappointment or betrayal. It can manifest in anxiety attacks as you see your bank account dwindle away, or it may be emotional pain, as with depression or physical pain, that completely knocks you flat on your back. Whatever kind of storm comes your way, pain is its natural companion.

I believe that one of the purposes of our storms is to become people of stronger faith. In order for that to happen, we have to stop fighting the storm and start embracing it as holy ground, as we discussed in a previous lesson. Now, don't get me wrong. I am not saying that you have to like it, but you do have to embrace the fact that it is here for a reason and will not go away until God's purpose is fulfilled. The first step toward healing is to stop running and to embrace this storm as a divine appointment scheduled by God Himself, just for you.

Our heavenly Father knows that the storms of life do the following:

- They make us stronger.
- They make us faithful Christians.
- They teach us to pour our hearts out in prayer.
- They cause a once unused Bible to become torn and tattered.

Fredina is my friend and colleague in ministry, and she prays the most beautiful, heartfelt prayers that are never her own words, but Holy Scripture poured out perfectly for whatever need she is praying.

I asked her one day, "How did you ever learn to pray like that?"

She said that she learned during a stormy time in her life when she found herself devouring her Bible and pouring her heart out in prayer. Her ability to pray these heartfelt prayers, with the Scripture memorized, is a gift that she carried out of the storm.

Wow—through the storms of life, Fredina learned to pray so eloquently that her prayers are now a blessing to all those who hear her pray.

Some lessons are only learned when we are in stormy weather, when God reveals aspects of His divine nature that broaden our awareness of Him. Here are ten things I have learned so far during the storms of life:

1. God is sovereign. We may not like His ways. We may not understand them. But we have to accept the fact that God has complete control over both heaven and earth.
2. Control is just an illusion. Every day of our lives is ordained and written in the Book of Life (Psalm 139:16). Being in a storm that is beyond our control confirms that being in control is just a mind game. Don't be fooled (take it from a previous control freak!).
3. Faith is only real once it has been tested. Through the fire, our faith is strengthened.
4. What doesn't kill you has the potential to make you stronger. This is the point of every storm.
5. Good in our eyes isn't always good in God's. To a sovereign God who sees the big picture, everything is good and fits into His perfect plan, whether we agree or not.
6. Life as we know it isn't promised to stay that way. God wants to remove us from our comfort zone and take us higher.
7. Everything counts. Nothing happens in vain. It all matters, and it all has purpose.
8. God hears our prayers, and He is speaking to us through our storms. The question is, Are we listening? Do we hear Him?
9. God is a loving God. Even when the storms are raging around us, He pours His amazing grace and mercy all over our lives.
10. Praise is meant in the good and in the bad. Praise God for who He is at *all* times.

Instead of continuing to run from this storm, I have decided to rest in the arms of God and trust Him.

Prayer

Father God, only You can help me to embrace this moment as a gift from You. I pray for your peace that surpasses all understanding and your joy that never ceases. In Jesus' name, I pray. Amen.

Meditation Song

Meditate on the lyrics to the song "Be Still and Know" by Steven Curtis Chapman.

Lesson 6

Storms Are Meant to Take Us Higher

Behold, I will do a new thing.
(Isaiah 43:19a KJV)

Have you ever had a friend who just changed on you? You know, the person just flipped the script on you. You thought everything was going well, but then, all of a sudden, things changed. You sat back and shook your head in disbelief.

That's what God just did to me. I thought I knew Him, but then He flipped the script and took our relationship to another level—without even consulting me! Clearly, He doesn't need my permission. I didn't realize it at first. In fact, it wasn't until I was dead-smack in the middle of it that I realized that things had changed.

I understand now that God allows situations to occur in my life to take me higher in my relationship with Him. But in order for that to happen, I have to go through *something* to get to that higher level. Often, we fight God's plan to take us higher. We get stuck along the way, asking God why this is happening to us.

I will admit that in the beginning of my storm, I spent way too much time asking God why. I mentioned before that God typically does not answer "why" questions, but I couldn't keep myself from asking. Of course, I received no answer. I eventually switched to asking, "When will this storm be over? When can I get back to my regular routine—you know, status quo, when all was well?"

Immediately, the Holy Spirit said, "Status quo? You think this storm was tailor-made for you to go back to life as it was? Really?"

In my mind, God was saying, "You got it twisted, and obviously you don't know Me as well as you claim to!"

Ouch!

It became clear that this storm was made specifically to speak to me and take me higher.

No more status quo! No more walking, talking, or living the same.

You see, going higher means that we gain a deeper understanding and walk closer with the Lord. It means that our faith is being refined to yield a higher praise. No more status quo!

Have I said it too much? Our storms have meaning and purpose.

When God takes your relationship to another level, He reveals Himself to you in ways that He hasn't before. Through the ups and downs of life, you experience new attributes of God that take your relationship to a new level, and this new level yields a deeper understanding of who He is.

The first time I ever experienced this was in 2007, when my apartment building caught fire and I lost every material thing I owned. I literally walked away with the pair of house slippers and the jogging suit I was wearing. I had recently moved into the apartment and was scheduled to purchase renter's insurance the following morning. Needless to say, I was not only devastated but also fearful about my future and about literally starting over from scratch. I had no idea how I was going to rebuild my life.

Then, God showed up and poured blessing after blessing after blessing, replacing everything and then some, within less than thirty days. *Wow!* Only God could do such a thing! During that season of my life, He took our relationship to a higher level. He revealed Himself as Jehovah Jireh—my provider. In my time of great need, He provided not just material things, but also a peace that surpassed all understanding. He provided comfort in the midst of fear. He remained true to His Word.

Here I am again with my health crisis, this seemingly never-ending pain. Even in this storm, I believe that God is taking me higher. This time, He is Jehovah Rapha—my healer. I didn't know Him like this before. I have only read about this attribute of God from the lives of the people in the Bible or from other people. Also, I witnessed it in family members, but I never experienced it personally. God has shown Himself to me in a new way. Even though my healing is not complete, God's grace is sufficient (2 Corinthians 12:9), and He still provides the breath of life for me. For that, I am grateful.

But in order to experience God in these new ways, I had to go to through the storms.

When God takes us higher, it is guaranteed that we will have to go through *it,* whatever *it* may be, to draw us closer to Him. In our going higher, God has to remove anything that is hindering us from going to the next level. This is a painful process; however, we have to trust that God knows the plans that He has for us (Jeremiah 29:11).

He allows the experiences of life to guide us toward walking into our divine purpose.

Be reassured that when storms come your way, it means that God is about to do a new thing in your life (Isaiah 43:19). It means that He is about to reveal Himself like you have never experienced before. Storms take us higher. Forget the status quo. You cannot embrace a storm and come out the same. God will not allow it.

Prayer

Sovereign God, there is none like You. I am grateful that I have You in the midst of this storm. Lord, please keep me close to Yourself and allow me to feel Your presence. Help me not to get caught up in my pain and disappointment, but to get caught up in You and Your promises. I know that You love me with an everlasting love, and I trust in You. In Jesus' name, I pray. Amen.

Meditation Song

Meditate on the lyrics to the song "You Raise Me Up" by Westlife.

Lesson 7

God Blesses Us in the Storms

> God blesses those who patiently endure testing and
> temptation. Afterward they will receive the crown of
> life that God has promised to those who love him.
> (James 1:12 NLT)

My health crisis initially presented as eye problems that required me to place steroid drops in my eyes every one to two hours and then to be seen by my ophthalmologist every two weeks. As the days passed, it did not seem that my eyes were healing. Of course, I started down the path of "what-if" questions. What if my eyes never healed? What if I lost my eyesight? What if I couldn't work anymore? The what-if questions led me down a path of unknowns that ultimately led to a great deal of unnecessary anxiety.

On top of that, other medical issues started popping up one right after the other. I found myself debilitated by pain and fatigue, and I had difficulty breathing. I had to be seen by multiple doctors on a weekly basis. I told my Bible study class that I was going to have to stop seeing all of these doctors because I thought they were the ones making me sick!

I was only half joking.

To make a very long story short, two months later I had finished the steroid eyedrops and was going to see my eye doctor for a follow-up appointment. As Murphy's Law would have it, the doctor was running behind. I found myself having to wait almost two hours for my appointment. I was in so much physical pain that I wanted to cry, but there were just too many people around for me to have a pity party. At the same time, I felt inconvenienced and upset about having to wait as long as I did. Yes (just in case you are wondering), I thought about rescheduling my appointment; however, my eyes were already dilated and I was not going to waste the time I had already waited.

So, I waited and waited …

Finally, I got in to see the doctor for a whopping five minutes. He said that my eyes had "quieted down" and that I could see him again in three months. My response to myself: *You had me wait two and a half hours for a five-minute exam for you to tell me that all is well?! Really?!*

I was a little heated, and I felt completely justified about being angry!

On my walk back to my car, the Holy Spirit said very loudly, "Did you hear what the doctor said? Your eyes are healed!"

I stopped dead in my tracks and said out loud, "Oh my, my eyes are healed!" I started laughing.

I'm sure that people on the street thought I was crazy. But it was a "wow" moment for me! I almost missed the blessing of my healing because I was distracted by my pain and was focused on having to wait for my appointment. I immediately thanked the Holy Spirit for that awakening.

That day, I was reminded that God is constantly pouring blessings all over our lives, even in the storms of life, yet we have to slow down if we are to see them. I almost missed God at work in my life. I almost missed the fact that He answered my prayers by healing my eyes.

We cannot become consumed with the blessings of yesterday or so focused on looking ahead for the blessings of tomorrow that we miss the blessing of today. Read that part again, and let it soak in for a minute. We tend to think that God hasn't blessed us because we find ourselves in the midst of stormy weather. Yet the truth is just the opposite. There are blessings all around us, but, because we are distracted by our circumstances, we miss the blessings, which are as follows:

- the gift of life
- the breath of life
- His provision for our daily needs
- His protection from hurt, harm, and danger
- the love of other people

And the list becomes longer when we focus on the blessings.

Blessings fall upon us every day.

There is an old story about a man who had two dogs living in him. One is loving, kind, and gentle, and the other is angry, mean, and ferocious. One day, the man's friend asked him which one was in control. The man simply replied, "The one I feed."

In other words, what we feed grows and is in control. What we give our attention to will dominate our thoughts and become the center of our actions.

I am suggesting that while in the storm, we take our focus off of our circumstances and use that energy to focus on all of the blessings God is pouring out on our lives. Do it now. Do it this very second.

The storehouses of heaven are always open, and they never run dry. Once we realize that we are on holy ground and embrace the idea that God is taking us higher, it becomes easier for our eyes to see all of the blessings around us.

Bottom line: It is not hard to see God's blessings when you want to see them.

Prayer

Father, thank You for the reminder that Your blessings are all around me. Thank You for giving me the gift of life and providing for every one of my needs according to Your good and perfect will. I find myself getting so distracted by my problems that I can miss Your provisions. Thank You for loving me and giving me exactly what I need the most—a closer walk with You. In Jesus' name, I pray. Amen.

Meditation Song

Meditate on the lyrics to the song "Blessings" by Laura Story.

Lesson 8

We Cannot Avoid Inner Work

Trust in the Lord with all of your heart and
lean not on your own understanding.
(Proverbs 3:5a NIV)

When we find ourselves in a storm, our first instinct is often to resist it, fight it, do whatever it takes to keep it from happening. But the reality is that we cannot stop it or make it end quickly. We do not have control over the circumstances that are happening all around and to us. The storm is actually beyond us, and it is bigger than we are.

Instead of fighting it, what we have to do is take a step back and ask those important questions that haunt us all:

- Why is this happening?
- Where did this come from?
- When will it end?
- What does it mean?

These questions haunt us because we don't have the answers. We wrestle with acceptance of this fact and become frustrated with the process, which is also much bigger than we are.

I believe that when we are in a storm, it is God speaking to us. It is also an invitation to look inward, inside of ourselves, and wrestle with what we think the answers to our questions are. This is what I refer to as inner work. Storms speak (and loudly!), but what are they saying to us personally? The kind of storm I am experiencing may be similar to your own, but I guarantee you that there is a different message for me than for you, and vice versa.

We have to learn how to see beyond what is directly in front of us—the pain, the heartache, the broken relationships, the inconvenience of our schedules, the negative impact on our finances, the sleepless nights. We are not to minimize those things, but we are not to stay focused on them, either. We have to get to the core of the storm: God is coming after our heart.

We must understand that the storm is not just outside of us, but also lying within us. We must pray that God first calms the storm within us to allow us to become grounded in Him so that we are then able to deal with the circumstances we are facing. If we try to do it the other way around, meaning that we deal with the circumstances and avoid the inner work, then we miss the point of the storm. And instead of growing, we become stagnant, not learning anything to help us move forward in our spiritual walk.

Trials teach us how to really lean on the everlasting arms of the Lord.

I believe that storms are proof, or evidence, that God sees us. Think back to your previous storms, and recall how God worked them out. Think back to the lessons you learned while in those storms, lessons that you would have never learned without the storm. You didn't know how God was going to work it out, but He did. You couldn't see Him working in those situations, but He was behind the scenes. And guess what? You made it through, even though you didn't think you would. Storms are God's handiwork, proof of His presence in

33

your life. They are confirmation of His love, which surpasses all understanding.

God gives us everything we need to weather the storms of life. We have a tendency to look around to find alternatives because, in our minds, inner work is difficult and requires too much effort. And we are correct: Inner work is difficult. But without it, we don't become stronger; instead, we become stagnant and bitter. The storms of life have purpose, but we have to endure those storms and lean on the Lord in order to gain insight into their meaning.

Sometimes, the storms come to gain our attention, to pull on our shirttail, to say, "Be still and know that I am God" (Psalm 46:10). In the busyness of life, we tend to forget that, so then God slows down life as we know it because our inner work is too important to be ignored.

Prayer

Lord, this is a tough lesson. Help me to do the work that is required to grow closer to You and become the person You created me to be. I cannot do this without You. Amen

Meditation Song

Meditate on the lyrics to the song "Draw Me Close" by Hillsong.

Lesson 9

We Must Praise God in the Storms

I will bless the Lord at all times: His praise
shall continually be in my mouth.
(Psalm 34:1 KJV)

I may not like my situation, but I am going to praise God anyhow!

I may not feel well right now, but I am going to praise Him anyhow!

Is there anybody willing to praise God on credit, because you remember where He has brought you from?

Is there anybody willing to praise God in advance for what He is going to do, because your faith tells you that your blessing is on the way, that your breakthrough is right around the corner?

Oh, but I am looking for the brave one who is willing to praise God right now—in the midst of your storm, in the midst of your heartache and disappointment, through your tears and pain.

Who is willing to praise God right now just because He is worthy to be praised?

The truth is that no matter where you find yourself, God is still God and is worthy to be praised!

Say this next line out loud: Oh, I will bless the Lord at all times—not some of the time, but all of the time.

Doesn't that feel good?

Often, I would say these words right before preaching so as to engage the audience in praise and worship. It would remind people that God is worthy of praise, no matter what.

In the midst of a challenging moment, these words came flooding into my head. The Holy Spirit convicted me and asked, "Will you praise God now? Will you praise Him in the midst of your pain and discouragement?"

My answer was, "Yes, I will praise the Lord at all times!"

You see, praise in the midst of our stormy weather confuses the Enemy. When we choose to praise God instead of remaining discouraged, the Enemy is taken off guard. When we choose praise over focusing on "O woe is me," the Enemy stumbles on his path. When we praise God and speak the Word of God in the midst of our tears, heartache, and disappointment, the Enemy has no choice but to flee from our presence.

Praising God Increases Our Faith

Your praise is saying the following to God: "Even though I cannot see my way and cannot feel Your presence, I am going to trust You anyhow. I am going to stand firmly on Your promises, from Genesis 1:1 to Revelation 22:21. I am going to hold onto

You and press forward, walking by faith and not by sight. I don't know how You are going to make a way, but I believe You are the way maker! I don't know when You will show up, but I know it will be right on time! And while I wait, I will praise You. I will sing of Your wondrous, mighty power. I will bless Your name in the storm and in the sunny weather! I will praise You at all times!"

As you continue to praise God, you will start to feel His presence. The Holy Spirit living inside of you can't help but shout, "Hallelujah!" The Holy Spirit can't help but praise God for who He is. Even when we find ourselves in the midst of stormy weather, we have to praise God, because the Holy Spirit reminds us of what He has done, even though our minds tend to forget.

The Holy Spirit can't help but praise God for what He is doing *and* for what He is going to do. He knows the importance of praising God in the midst of our storms. When we should be down and out, losing our minds and going crazy, praise strengthens our faith and allows us to persevere through the ups and downs of life.

While praising God in the midst of a very painful moment, the phrase "stronger faith, higher praise" came to my mind over and over again. I realized that, once again, God was speaking. He was teaching and showing me how He was working. And it is true: The stronger my faith, the higher my praise—and the higher my praise, the stronger my faith becomes.

God is absolutely amazing! Funny, I thought I already knew that. I thought I had a pretty good relationship with Him, yet He never ceases to amaze me. Once again, He shot the ball out of the park and went above and beyond all that I could ever ask or imagine. I am praising God in the midst of this storm because He has remained faithful to His Word and has walked with me every step of the way.

In the midst of our storms, we have to praise God anyhow!

Prayer

Lord, I will bless Your name through the good and the bad times. Thank You for who You are. You are worthy of all of praise! Thank You for life as I know it. Thank You for loving me in this storm. To You be all the glory, majesty, and praise, today and forevermore! Amen.

Meditation Song

Meditate on the lyrics to the song "Praise Is What I Do" by William Murphy.

Lesson 10

Getting Rest Is Important

The Lord replied, "My Presence will go
with you, and I will give you rest."
(Exodus 33:14 NIV)

"Honey, you should get some rest." I've heard this over and over again recently as I've been struggling with my health crisis.

Rest?! I've thought to myself. *All I've been doing is resting!*

With as much rest as I have gotten, I should be Superwoman, flying around the world with a blue cape on my back and a big *S* emblazoned on my chest. Seriously!

I have literally gone from the couch in the living room to the couch in my office or to my bed, and then back to the couch in the living room, starting the rotation all over again.

Inside, I am screaming, *I don't need more rest! Instead, I need to get up and start moving and being productive* [my favorite word]!

Clearly, my body had a different agenda. In my mind, I wanted to move and be productive, but my body would insist on sleeping for hours—days, it seemed. I would wake up five hours later in the same position, not having accomplished a single thing but rest.

One day, my aunt asked me, "Are you really resting?"

I thought, *Of course I am. I am lying on the couch in the same exact position for hours. I think I've got this resting thing down pat.*

But as I stepped back and really listened to her question, I realized that there is a difference between lying on the couch for hours and truly resting.

What I found myself doing while lying on the couch was replaying every negative experience I'd had since becoming ill. I replayed over and over again, silently in my head, every conversation at the doctor's office describing the details of my pain. Recalling all the details, I ruminated over all of the things on my to-do list that were not getting done. So, my muscles were tensed, and I was gritting my teeth and clenching my fists, all while "resting" on the couch. My body was nowhere near resting. My mind was full of anxiety and fear. I was quietly reliving my horror movie over and over, which intensified my pain and any negative emotions I was experiencing.

I learned that in order to truly rest, I had to quiet my mind. I had to learn to consciously relax my body. I had to learn to get to a place of healing so I could find peace and quietly rest my mind, calm my heart, and, yes, relax my body.

We must remember that the mind, body, and spirit are connected. What the mind thinks is manifested through the body. So, if my mind is chaotic, then how in the world do I expect my body to heal and "rest"? It will not. And any efforts I make toward healing will be in vain.

Scripture tells us not to be anxious (Philippians 4:6) and to take captive every thought (2 Corinthians 10:5). I started doing this intentionally by meditating on the Scriptures and literally controlling my thoughts to achieve a relaxed, focused state. Meditating on the words of my favorite Scripture replaced the rerun of my horror movie. Scripture meditation moved me toward a deep state of relaxation, one that I can control. I cannot control my situation, but I can control how I respond to it.

As I enter into a deeper level of rest, I not only relax my body but also release hormones and endorphins to calm my heart rate, lower my blood pressure, and release any muscle tension. This allows my body to truly rest and my spirit to become more settled.

When we are in "autopilot mode" (lesson thirteen), we don't really rest, as it is a natural human instinct to replay one's horror movie over and over again. The upsetting scenes are stored in the memory bank, and, in some strange way, the review brings us comfort—uncomfortable comfort. We have to intentionally shift to "Holy Spirit–pilot mode."

We Have to Want to Change Our Thoughts

Sometimes, it is easier to stay in the storm than to move beyond it. As we discussed previously, inner work entails some hard work. Lying on the couch for several hours and having a pity party was easier for me than changing my thought process or venturing down a path of unknowns. I get that. But common sense tells me to try something else when what I'm doing doesn't work. So, I did that. And I got better results.

Are you willing to try something different? Are you willing to do whatever it takes to get through the storm in a healthy, productive way? Are you willing to go after your healing or go after your blessing?

If you are going to rest, then at least get some quality rest. It is a bonus that when meditating, you don't even have to get up off the couch!

Prayer

Lord, help me to find rest and peace within Your Word and in Your presence. Help me not to be anxious or tense about the circumstances of my life but, instead, to trust in You. In Jesus' name, I pray. Amen.

Meditation Song

Meditate on the lyrics to the song "Praise You in this Storm" by Casting Crowns.

Lesson 11

It Really Is Okay to Cry
with Someone

Jesus wept.
(John 11:35 NIV)

"It is okay to cry. You just had a stroke and your life has changed. Just cry and let it out."

I said these words on numerous occasions years ago when I worked as a nurse on a stroke unit. I would tell my patients that if they didn't cry, then they would get fat from holding inside the tears that were screaming to get out. The women would laugh. However, to my surprise, the men would burst into tears. I found myself sitting quietly with these men while they expressed whatever they were feeling.

It is amazing how easy it was for me to tell my patients just to let their feelings out and cry. Yet, I didn't allow myself to do the same thing when facing my own health crisis. Why? Perhaps I had become so accustomed to hiding my tears and crying alone.

So, you can imagine that this lesson was big for me. I had to learn to let go of whatever dysfunctional thoughts I had about crying in front of other people, and I had to give myself the gift of crying out loud with someone. I had to allow myself a moment of transparency and vulnerability to find out that there is something refreshing when one cries with someone else.

My moment came one day while my best friend, Marcie, was visiting. I was having difficulty getting up off of the sofa, and my tears just started quietly flowing. I could not believe that I was crying in front of her.

It was so freeing.

Author and columnist Regina Brett has a chapter in her book *God Never Blinks* on this very topic. The name of the chapter is "Cry with Someone. It's More Healing than Crying Alone." She writes that the best advice she ever received on crying was to cry with someone else. Her therapist told her that crying alone isn't as powerful as crying with another person. Brett goes on to say, "Cry alone and you'll keep crying those same tears over and over. Cry with someone and those tears have the power to heal you once and for all."[4]

This is great advice for us all.

Allowing yourself to feel whatever you feel at the moment is part of the healing process in the storm. We tend to try to be strong for everyone else around us, but I believe that everyone around us would love to have permission to cry, especially with the person who is in the storm. Trust me: When your friends and family are alone, they cry out for you, so why not have a good, hearty cry together? End it with a big sigh of relief or a big laugh, and then move on to the next moment.

Prayer

Lord, thank You for reminding me that it is okay to cry and to let my emotions show. I know that I am safe in Your arms and that You accept me right where I am. Thank You for blessing me with people who love and care about me and who are willing to laugh and, yes, cry with me. You are an awesome God, and I love You for giving me just what I need, exactly when I need it. Amen.

Meditation Song

Meditate on the lyrics to the song "He Has His Hands on You" by Marvin Sapp.

Lesson 12

Storms Are Invitations,
Not Interruptions

Every good and perfect gift is from above, coming
down from the Father of the heavenly lights.
(James 1:17a NIV)

Some might view a storm as an interruption. To be transparent for
a minute, I admit that that was my initial response. *I don't have time
for this. There is too much work to do. I have people to see, places to go,
things to check off and add to my never-ending to-do lists! This is just not
a good time!*

But would any time be good?

As I fought every hour of every day for the storm not to happen, I
found myself exhausted and experiencing more intense pain.

Hmm … was I making matters worse by my attitude? Absolutely!
In fact, the more I fought, the worse my situation seemed to get. It
wasn't until I calmed down and started letting go that things started
to change. This situation reminds me of a card that I have framed on
my wall. The card, which my friend Danielle gave me years ago, says,
"Let go and let God," and it shows a picture of two ladies dancing. I

believe they are dancing because they have just given their problems over to God and are feeling free of their burdens.

I learned to stop worrying and to start trusting in God.

I finally got to a place of embracing my situation as a divine invitation directly from God. In a weird way, I got excited to see what God was going to do. In my eyes, this storm meant that God really did see me and that He had tailor-made this season in my life to speak directly to me. It meant that He actually orchestrated this time off from my somewhat chaotic routine so that I could just sit at His feet to learn more about Him, more about myself, and more about the gift of life.

When God first presented this awesome opportunity, it appeared to be an inconvenience, a terrible interruption of my ministry, an unwanted detour, a nerve-wracking, fearful, and frustrating moment. But as it lingered and evolved, my eyes were opened to something bigger—something beyond me.

It became clear that this was something spiritual.

I realized that God was speaking (loudly!). I almost missed it because I was consumed with my pain. I was so overwhelmed with what was going on with me physically that I almost missed what was going on spiritually. I almost missed hearing God in the midst of my storm.

I am thankful that God is persistent and that He doesn't give up even when we don't pay Him any attention. He continues pursuing us. I speculate that my healing didn't come as quickly as I would have liked (who likes waiting?!) because, perhaps, I didn't hear what God was saying. I was distracted, caught up in my own pity party.

The pain lingered, questions went unanswered, and days turned into weeks—and weeks into months. God came back in the still, small voice, and this time I heard Him loud and clear: "Keep your eyes on Me, listen, and be still."

In an article titled "Invisible Heroics," author Erin Gieschen writes, "We see affliction as obstacles rather than a gift or tool that can make us who we are meant to be."[5] I know I sound like a broken record, but I can't say it enough: All storms have purpose and meaning. What I considered an interruption was the best invitation I ever received.

Prayer

Father God, I am so thankful that my initial impression was not my last impression, because my attitude almost hindered me from moving forward through this storm. But You knew that I would respond this way, because You know me better than I know myself. Thank You for Your patience and long suffering in dealing with me. Thank You for this invitation to draw closer to You. Help me through this storm, so that I may grow and become stronger in my walk with You. In Jesus' name, I pray. Amen.

Meditation Song

Meditate on the lyrics to the song "Falling in Love with Jesus" by Jonathan Butler and Kirk Whalum.

Lesson 13

The Holy Spirit Is Our Pilot in the Storms

But the Counselor, the Holy Spirit, whom
the Father will send in my name, will
teach you all things and will remind you
of everything I have said to you.
(John 14:26 NIV)

Before Jesus ascended to heaven, He promised to send us a "Helper" (John 14:26 NCV) to help us navigate through life.

That helper is the Holy Spirit. We automatically receive the Holy Spirit when we confess our sins, believe that Jesus is the Son of God, and invite Him to come live in our hearts. God knew that we would need help, so He gave us an awesome gift, one that is with us at *all* times, in the sunshine and in the storm.

When we wake up and find ourselves in stormy weather, we have to understand that with it comes a great deal of work. We have to work on our attitude, we have to work on seeing our blessings, we have to work on praising God, and we have to stop running from the storm. There is so much work we have to do in order to weather the storms of life. Oftentimes, we miss the work (which is really a benefit of the storm) because we are distracted or consumed by the problem itself.

So, how do we accomplish all of the work required?

It is only through the power of the Holy Spirit.

With the power of the Holy Spirit, much like the muscle strength we achieve through exercise, we build and sustain the strength of our faith by shifting our focus to God's Word and His promises. We have to shift our mind off autopilot mode ("O woe is me"), our natural mind, to Holy Spirit–pilot mode ("I can do all things through Christ who strengthens me" [Philippians 4:13]), a supernatural mind.

When we are in autopilot mode, we do what comes naturally: We cry, complain to anyone who will listen, stay angry, stay frustrated, don't eat, withdraw, and go crazy by replaying our horror movie. It's a result of our natural mind, which is controlled by the flesh.

When we are in Holy Spirit–pilot mode, we cry tears of pain and tears of joy; we take our complaints to the Lord in prayer; we learn to praise in spite of the heartache; we—yes, even through the tears—see the blessings all around us; and we devour the Bible and find inspiration in new-to-us Scriptures that we never read or absorbed before (for me, this was Psalm 71). We often find new meaning in our favorite Scriptures. We welcome visits from old friends and new friends, who are there to pray with us and help in any way they can.

Being in Holy Spirit mode, we grow through the storms of life, which allows us to mature in our relationship with Christ. I am reminded of the quotation from Charles Stanley mentioned in lesson two.

When the Holy Spirit is leading us, the following things happen:

- We start to mature and see our situation through a new set of lenses.
- We start to embrace the storm instead of fighting against it.
- We start to trust God instead of doubting His ways.
- We start to move toward a state of contentment and thankfulness instead of grumbling and wasting time, wishing things were different.

This is not to say that when we are in Holy Spirit–pilot mode we don't revert to autopilot mode. We do, over and over, but it does not become the center of our focus. We can't stay there, as the Holy Spirit will not allow it.

But trust me: We visit there often.

Please don't misunderstand: This transformation doesn't happen overnight. It only happens through a daily process of prayer, fasting, and surrendering to the Holy Spirit. In my experience, I flipped back and forth from autopilot mode to Holy Spirit–pilot mode, and then back to autopilot mode. Many days I spent on autopilot, singing the "O woe is me" sad song. It was like a roller-coaster ride: I was going up and down. Sometimes, I found myself at a standstill, not knowing who was in control.

Even though we have *all* of the Holy Spirit at the moment when we become believers, the reality is that the Holy Spirit does not have *all of us*—and that is why we can flip from autopilot mode to being driven by the Holy Spirit.

We choose our pilot in the storms.

Unfortunately, I am as moody as they come. One moment, I am fine and praising God. The next moment, I am yelling, "Why is this happening?" In order to be driven by the Holy Spirit, we have to submit and surrender to His leading. We have to pray and read the Word of God. We have to let God be God in our lives and in this storm.

Prayer

Almighty God, You know me better than I know myself. You know how I am going to respond to life's circumstances before I do. I admit that sometimes I surrender to the Holy Spirit, and other times I fight Him. Thank You for your patience as I grow. Lord, help me through this storm. I don't know when it will end, and I don't know what will happen next. But You do. So, I trust in You, and I pray for a fresh indwelling of the Holy Spirit to guide me when I am overwhelmed and feeling the weight on my shoulders. I know that I can lay everything at Your feet and trust that You will handle my cares. Lord, I love You with all of my heart, and I thank You for being with me during every moment of every day. In Jesus' name, I pray. Amen.

Meditation Song

Meditate on the lyrics to the song "Jesus, Savior, Pilot Me."

Lesson 14

We Have to Trust the Process

"For my thoughts are not your thoughts, neither
are your ways my ways," saith the Lord.
(Isaiah 55:8 KJV)

Have you ever played Klondike Solitaire? For those of you who have not, the goal of the game is to get all of the cards from seven piles into four piles. The cards in the seven piles can be moved by counting downward and alternating colors. For example, a five of hearts (red) can only go on a six of spades or a six of clubs (black). However, the four piles count upward and can only go in sequence. For example, the five of hearts can only go on a four of hearts.

Got it?

I will admit that I am hooked on the game. In fact, I have an app on my cell phone that I absolutely love. Anytime I find myself waiting, I pull out my phone and get lost in the game. I have gotten so quick at playing that I can play about five games in less than ten minutes.

One day while playing, I had the option of moving either a five of clubs or a five of spades. I could not move them both, so I had to choose, but which one? I opted to move the five of clubs to the six of diamonds, and I smiled when I flipped over the next card, which was a six of hearts. This meant that I was able to move the five of spades, too. Yay for me!

All I had to do was trust the process.

As I continued to play the game, that thought kept coming to me: *Trust the process.*

And I thought to myself, *Isn't this the same lesson in life? Trust the process, especially when we find ourselves in a storm? Isn't it the same when we can't see our way out of our current situation or when our situation seems to be getting the best of us? Aren't we to trust that God is working out our situation, even though we cannot see anything working out in our favor or figure out the next step to take?*

We have to just trust the process and remember that in all things, good and bad, God is working it out according to His perfect plan. Often, in the storms of life, we have to regroup and shift our focus. We literally have to let go and let God work out the situation on our behalf.

My dear friend Kristin sent me a quotation by Neal A. Maxwell that is perfect for this lesson: "Faith in God includes faith in His timing." In other words, if we are going to have faith in almighty God that He can do anything but fail, then we should also have faith that His timing and the duration of our storms are for a far greater purpose. Our job is simply to trust His process.

Now, this is really simple, but sometimes we flip to the other side of trust, which is worry. Is anybody guilty of that (or is it just me)?

When we stop trusting in God's process, we start worrying about our circumstances. Not seeing a clear outcome, we start to maneuver and manipulate our circumstances, trying to help God out. God doesn't need our help in accomplishing His plans. The fact is that the more we worry, the farther away we get from trusting and the farther away we get from God.

This is where we get into trouble.

We start believing that God does not see our problems because He is not responding quickly enough. We start to think that perhaps our long list of problems is too big for Him to handle. Or worse yet, we start to believe that God doesn't care enough about us to be concerned about what concerns us.

The Scripture says that God's ways are not our ways and that His thoughts are not ours (Isaiah 55:8). It also says that in this world, we will have trials, troubles, tribulations, and raging storms, but we are to take comfort in Jesus, the Son of God, who came to conquer all of our fears and concerns. We are not to be anxious about anything (Philippians 4:6).

All we are to do is trust the process.

Everything in life has meaning. God is using our experiences for His purpose—to fulfill His good and perfect will. We never want to miss the lessons in the storms of life, because they have the power to change our lives forever. When you are in a storm of any kind, you learn that it isn't about you. Yes, you physically have to go through it, but it really is all about God and what He is going to work out through you so that you may glorify Him and draw others unto Him.

It is not about you or me—we are just the vessels being used for a higher purpose. And we will reap the benefits from the blessing on the other side of the storm (and in the midst of them!). You, my friend, just have to trust the process and believe that God knows what He is doing.

Prayer

Father, once again You make it simple—trust in Your process, trust in Your ways, trust in Your Word, simply trust in You. Today, with the power of the Holy Spirit, I will trust in You and not in myself or in how I think my circumstances should work out. I will trust in You today and always. And Lord, when I start to waver, please bring me back to where I need to be. In Jesus' name, I pray. Amen.

Meditation Song

Meditate on the lyrics to the song "I Trust You" by James Fortune.

Lesson 15

In Your Storm, Pray for Someone Else

For this reason, since the day we heard about
you, we have not stopped praying for you.
(Colossians 1:9a NIV)

May we be transparent for a moment?

Are you guilty of saying that you will pray for someone, but, when the time comes to pray, you can't remember who or what you were supposed to pray about?

If we are honest with ourselves and with each other, then we will acknowledge that this happens more than we would like to admit.

It used to happen to me way too often because my head was so cluttered with my never-ending to-do list that I would lose people's prayer requests. So, to make sure that I kept my word to the other person, I got into the habit of praying with the person right on the spot or while I was walking away or hanging up the phone.

Praying for someone else is an awesome gift that we cannot take for granted.

During my own storm, I have spent many nights, too many nights, lying on the floor and crying out to God to relieve my pain and give me the strength to endure this storm another night. One night while I was crying out, the Holy Spirit laid my friend Gayle on my heart. He kept bringing her name to my mind and impressed upon me that I should pray for her. This happened on several occasions. Instead of continuing to pray for myself, I shifted my focus to praying for Gayle.

You see, Gayle was fighting a battle with cancer and was told by her doctors that there was nothing else to be done. She had undergone all the treatments available, but the cancer was too aggressive and was spreading in her body. It was time to move her to hospice.

I speculate that during my painful nights, God presented Gayle in my spirit so that I would pray for her through her painful days and nights. He wanted to remind me that this storm wasn't just about me and that there were many people in my life who were also suffering. So, every night that I was up with pain, I would pour out my heart for Gayle like I was praying for myself. I prayed and asked God to comfort her and her family and to walk with them through this storm that threatened everything they held dear. I never got a chance to share this with Gayle before the Lord called her home, but I believe that the Lord answered my prayers.

Prayer is the greatest gift we can give to someone when life isn't working out as we had hoped. When we say we are going to pray, we must keep our word. I am thankful for the prayer warriors whom God has placed in my life, people who go boldly to the throne of God on my behalf. My heart is warmed for the many people for whom I do the same without their even knowing.

In order to really embrace this particular lesson, please stop and pray for whomever the Lord lays on your heart at this moment. Make a list of those who are in need of prayer, and pray for them so as to lift them up as you lift up yourself.

Prayer

Jesus, You died on the cross and rose from the dead so that we would have direct access to God, our Father. I come to You on behalf of [insert name], that You would bless them according to their specific need. I do not know exactly what they need, but You do. I come standing in the gap for them, asking You to strengthen and guide them through life. Lord, draw them in closer to You; protect and keep them just like You do for me. In Jesus' name, I pray. Amen.

Meditation Song

Meditate on the lyrics to the song "What Faith Can Do" by Kutless.

Lesson 16

We Have to Keep Moving

Being confident of this, that he who began
a good work in you will carry it on to
completion until the day of Christ Jesus.
(Philippians 1:6 NIV)

During my season of pain, many well-meaning people told me to stop preaching and teaching Bible study. They would quote Psalm 46:10, asking me to "just be still"—for once already!

However, I couldn't.

For one, I had given my word about these commitments. Unless the Lord told me to cancel, I believed that He would give me the strength to follow through with them. And once I received the message that I was to preach or teach, that served for me as confirmation to keep moving.

Second, I needed to preach and teach because it was an encouragement for my spirit. It helped me to focus on others and not be consumed with "me, me, me." The messages were so inspiring that, as I prepared them, I literally felt uplifted and encouraged.

More important, I was actually experiencing what I was teaching. For example, I had just started teaching a women's Bible study class at church, using the book *Discerning the Voice of God* by Priscilla Shirer. This study was about hearing and discerning the voice of God in our personal lives. The lesson I was to teach the week I got sick was about waiting for God to answer prayers. Wow, that is exactly where I found myself waiting—waiting for my healing, waiting for relief, waiting for God to show up and wipe all of my pain away. It was not a mistake that this was the lesson I was scheduled to teach. As I prepared the lesson, I shared with my sisters not only what was in the study guide, but also what I was doing personally during my illness.

God's timing is amazing. He had me right where He wanted me. The teaching was personal.

Then, I had another opportunity to preach, one that had been on my calendar for months. Everyone thought I should cancel. Once again, I said that I had not received the message to cancel and that God had given me such a beautiful message that He would give me the strength to deliver it.

I just needed someone to pick me up because, since I had been sick, I learned that God only gives me the strength to do what He has for me at that moment. Afterward, I deflate like a balloon—and the pain comes on like a monster. So, as long as someone was willing to drive me, I was willing to go.

This particular preaching opportunity was at a women's prison. I had never been in a women's prison and, to be honest, wasn't sure I wanted to go. I was afraid of going into that environment. I had volunteered at a juvenile detention center before, which was okay for some reason, probably because it was young girls and teenagers who were not as frightening in my mind as adult women who were incarcerated for all kinds of crimes. But let me tell the truth and shame the Devil: I had run away from this opportunity on more than one occasion, but since I had started preaching, I promised God that I would not run away from any opportunity He gave me.

So, I had to keep moving.

The message for this prison ministry spoke deep to my heart, given all the pain I was experiencing. It was no mistake that I was where I was spiritually, mentally, and physically. When I delivered this message, it was with such sincerity and conviction. I was speaking from a place of experience, not about something I had read or heard from someone else. God knew the timing of my storm and the timing of this prison ministry message. Of course, it worked according to His plan.

The day before I was scheduled to preach, one of my best friends, Genya, was visiting and asked me what I was preaching about. I told her about the Scripture in Isaiah 41:8–10 and the highlights of the message. I said to her that these women needed to know that God had not forgotten about them. Genya said, "That is the same thing God is saying to you: He has not forgotten about you."

How many times do you think, because you have no relief from your storm, that God has forgotten about you? That lie comes into my head, especially at night when I am all alone and crying out in pain. It may be a lie, but it comes at me like it is the truth. I have to pray like never before to combat that lie in my mind. I have to sing, praise, and allow the Holy Spirit to literally fight the battle going on in my head.

Wherever you find yourself, don't you dare start believing the lies of the Enemy. Don't you dare think for a moment that God has forgotten about you or that He does not hear your cries. He hears every one of them, and He promises never to leave you or forsake you (Deuteronomy 31:6b).

Prayer

Almighty God, please allow me to keep moving forward and holding onto Your hand. Your Word says that when I am weak, that is when Your strength is made perfect. Lord, please show me how to glorify You in all that I say and do, especially during this difficult time. Every day that You give me is a blessing, and I want to please You with my life. In Jesus' name, I pray. Amen.

Meditation Song

Meditate on the lyrics to the song "Walk by Faith" by Jeremy Camp.

Lesson 17

Jesus Sticks Closer
than a Brother

A friend loves at all times, and a
brother is born for adversity.
(Proverbs 17:17 NIV)

Jesus is the only one who can go through this time with you. I am reminded of the time when the disciples were in a storm in the middle of the Sea of Galilee. You can read the passage in the Gospel of Matthew, 14:22–32.

Once you have read the passage, ask yourself this simple question: Who sent the disciples out by boat? It was Jesus. I find it interesting that Jesus was the one who sent the disciples by boat to get to the other side of the sea.

I heard a sermon once about this passage. The minister posed the question, "If Jesus knew that there was a storm coming, then why did He choose to send the disciples into the sea, directly into the storm?" He speculated that there were lessons that the disciples could only learn by being in a boat that was tossed back and forth by the waves in the sea. Only then could Peter learn that if he kept his eyes on Jesus, he, too, could walk on water.

Some lessons are only learned in the storm.

What I find comforting about this particular passage is not that Peter was able to walk on water, but that Jesus was right there in the eye of the storm, walking toward the disciples in the boat.

Jesus was right there.

This offers me the reassurance that when I am out on the stormy seas of life, Jesus, my Savior, is right there with me.

We have to believe with all of our heart that God guides us through the storm, not from afar, but by holding our hand. In order to touch our hand, He has to be in close contact with us. Nobody else sticks closer to us than Jesus does.

You have your family and close friends who pray for you, help you, visit with you, cry with you, and go with you to important appointments. But not one of them can actually feel your heartache, feel your pain, wrestle with your inner thoughts, or wrap his or her hand around your inner heart. Nobody can do that but God. And He says, I am your strength, your refuge, and I will never leave you nor forsake you (Hebrews 13:5). God says, "I will be with you in this storm."

We must remember that God is not only the storm maker, but He is also the one who calms the storm by just speaking a word. Remember how He quieted the storm faced by the disciples by saying, "Quiet, be still" (Mark 4:39)? But also note that, again, He was there with His disciples, right in the eye of the storm.

What a comfort in the midnight hour, when your body is covered in pain, your mind is racing a mile a minute, and your tears are flowing like a waterfall, to know that God is there, wrapping His arms around you, wiping every tear and catching the ones that fall in His hands. He is there when everyone else goes home to continue praying. He is there in the quiet of the night when your mind seems to go crazy in every direction with what-if questions. Just as He was there with the disciples out on the stormy seas, He is walking faithfully with us, His children.

Prayer

God, You are absolutely amazing. Thank You for being the One who remains with me like no other. In this storm, I find comfort in the fact that You are walking close beside me and holding my hand. Lord, words cannot express how grateful I am that the God of the universe sees me and cares about me. I know that it is only because of the blood of Jesus that I am able to walk in close and intimate fellowship with You. Jesus, thank You for sacrificing Your life, that I may be able to weather the storms of my life. I am holding onto the hope that can only come from You. In Jesus' name, I pray. Amen.

Meditation Song

Meditate on the lyrics to the song "He Has His Hands on You" by Marvin Sapp.

Lesson 18

God Will Have His Way

Then the Lord sent a great wind on the sea, and such a
violent storm arose that the ship threatened to break up.
(Jonah 1:4 NIV)

The storms of life are inevitable; no one is exempt from them. When
they come, we often wonder what God is up to. We wonder what
the purpose of our pain is and what good, if any, can come out of
our adversity. In order to get some insight, we have to remember
that storms come our way from many different sources. Following
are four sources through which storms enter our lives.

Satan's Plan: According to the Scriptures, our Enemy prowls
around, seeking whom he can devour. He has a plan to destroy our
credibility and our relationship with Jesus Christ. His ultimate goal
is to fill our lives with so much discouragement and worry that we
cannot focus on Jesus and the purpose He has for our lives.

Fallen World: As people of faith, we are not exempt from the
troubles of this world. We receive the gift of the Holy Spirit the
moment we accept Christ into our lives, which allows us to have
supernatural power to face the trials and troubles of our lives. This
power gives us joy and hope that goes beyond our circumstances. In

order to know that God's grace is sufficient, we have to endure trials and tribulations, just like nonbelievers do.

God's Will: Our almighty God is in control of everything, and He knows that our lowest, darkest moments can be our greatest blessings. He allows adversity to mold us into what He created us to be.

Our Fault: Simply put, sometimes we are the source of our own storms because we disobey a direct command from God. We want our own way; therefore, we disregard God's instructions. We don't trust God's way, so we try to do it our way and find ourselves in a mess that we created.

This is what happened to the prophet Jonah. God gave him a direct command to go and warn the people of Nineveh, and Jonah said no and then proceeded to run in the opposite direction. God told him to go east, but Jonah went west. Then, almighty God sent a storm to stop Jonah in his tracks, to remind him that, ultimately, He is in control of our lives.

Has God ever done that to you? Is this storm you are facing caused by your running, your disobedience? Perhaps God has told you to do something that you aren't too keen on doing—let go of a relationship, get rid of a habit, change jobs, put Him first in your finances, forgive someone who has hurt you, or go somewhere you don't want to go. Whatever it is, you can learn from Jonah: There isn't anywhere you can run from God. He is the Creator of heaven and earth and everything in it. He will find you and send a storm in your life to get your attention.

Yet, even if this storm is because of our disobedience, we must not lose heart. While Jonah fled, God pursued. While Jonah was disobedient, God's grace and mercy prevailed. The storm God sent was actually a blessing. The big fish that swallowed Jonah actually saved his life and got him back on track. In the belly of the fish, Jonah prayed. He repented. He turned back to God.

And we can do the same.

As we are His children, God is faithful to us, even when the storms of life are our own doing, the direct consequence of our disobedience and sin. He is faithful to discipline us with love and then welcome us back home. No matter the reason for the storm, there is nowhere we can go where God isn't. He will lead us and guide us back to the path that He has set for us. We must remember the quotation from Charles Stanley mentioned in lesson two, saying that the storms of life are not meant to overtake us or to destroy our spirit, but to teach us and to mold us—to be what God created us to be. It is God's way of calling us back to Him.

We cannot make the mistake of thinking that God will not forgive us. We cannot get stuck in thinking that our disobedience has removed us so far from His presence. The Scriptures tell us that there is nowhere we can go that His love can't find us (Psalm 139). There is no storm that can come into our lives that can keep us from God. Let me stress that again: Nothing, not one thing, can separate us from the love of Christ!

> For I am convinced that neither death nor life, neither angels nor demons, neither the present nor the future, nor any powers, neither height nor depth, nor anything else in all creation, will be able to separate us from the love of God that is in Christ Jesus our Lord. (Romans 8:38–39)

In your quiet meditative time, read the book of Jonah. As you read it, picture the love of God pouring out onto your life like it did on Jonah's. See a merciful God meeting you where you are and gently bringing you back into relationship with Him. God was merciful toward Jonah, and He regards us the same. While the book of Jonah details a storm that was the result of Jonah's complete disobedience to a direct command from God, it also proves that the detours we take don't alter God's plan. In the end, we wind up right where we are supposed to be.

Prayer

Father God, thank You for loving me in spite of my sin and disobedience. Thank You for showering me with Your love, Your grace, and Your mercy. Thank You for "bringing my life up from the pit" (Jonah 2:6b). Thank You for bringing me back home to You. Your love for me is beyond my understanding. I am grateful for another chance to live life according to Your good and perfect plan. Thank You. In Jesus' name, I pray. Amen.

Meditation Song

Meditate on the lyrics to the song "East to West" by Casting Crowns.

Lesson 19

Storms Make Us Take Off Our Masks

Come to me, all who are weary and
burdened, and I will give you rest.
(Matthew 11:28 NIV)

During Halloween, many children are excited about getting lots of candy and wearing their favorite costumes and masks. Many children dress up as their favorite superhero or fairy-tale princess. But once the parties and trick-or-treating are over, it's time to take off the costumes, put the masks down, and get back to reality.

Is this easier said than done? Perhaps our reality is wearing masks, hiding our true self behind our masks every day. Perhaps we have grown so accustomed to wearing our masks that we don't even realize that we have them on.

What exactly do I mean by wearing masks?

- Pretending that all is well when it really isn't.
- Pretending that we are handling the circumstances of our lives without needing help.

- Pretending that we aren't overwhelmed with all that is around us when we are really barely holding on.
- Pretending that we have forgiven someone while harboring bitterness and anger in our heart.

We wear masks to protect ourselves, to hide our true feelings. Oftentimes, we have worn them for so long that they have become a part of who we are. Sometimes, masks are needed to help us get through a stormy season in our lives.

But they become a problem when we put them on every day instead of dealing with the issues that overwhelm our minds and hearts. Wearing a mask becomes an issue when we are not being real with our loved ones or ourselves. The mask starts to harm us rather than help us if we never take it off, if we never let our guard down and just be real.

Here are a few types of masks that we wear:

1. "All is well" mask: Our world is crumbling, but we are too embarrassed to share.
2. "Got it going on" mask: We have the house, the job, the car, the material things, and the relationship, but we continue to feel empty and unfulfilled inside.
3. "Nothing bothers me" mask: We pretend as if we are not hurting, as if we have thick skin, yet we harbor bitterness and resentment every day.
4. "Happy-go-lucky" mask: We pretend to be happy all the time, yet we are struggling with depression or an anxiety disorder.

When we wear our masks, pretending that all is well, we miss out on the support and love we need to deal with our problems. This places us on an island, of sorts. We isolate ourselves from growing, and we become stagnant, bitter, and distracted by living in a vicious cycle of regret and blame. This is the worst position to be in when we are facing a storm.

We are not meant to walk the journey of life alone, nor are we meant to suffer alone.

We have to get off of the treadmill of life and take some time to reflect on our true feelings, the real motives behind our actions, and ask the following questions: "Is this the real me?" "Is this the best me that I can be?"

Just as children become exhausted when they come back from trick-or-treating, we get exhausted when carrying our unnecessary baggage. Just like some children don't want to take off their costumes and masks at the end of the day, we also get so comfortable wearing our masks that we want to sleep in them and wear them the next day. We end up feeling completely worn out.

As people of faith, we do not have to walk around wearing masks, pretending that all is well when it is not. We can be overwhelmed with life's circumstances and still have joy. Everything around us can be falling apart, but we can still have peace and hold onto hope for a better day.

"But how?" you may ask. We always have to look at our relationship with God; His Son, Jesus; and the Holy Spirit. Ultimately, we have to look to the Word of God.

God says to come to Him as you are and to take off your masks and be real. He already knows what burdens you carry; He already knows what baggage you bring and what hurts your heart. You see, the human being looks at the outside, but God looks on the inside, at our hearts. He knows it all. And His Word says, "Come to me, all who are weary and burdened, and I will give you rest" (Matthew 11:28 NIV). He says to come and seek whatever it is you need so that you can find peace and rest while living in this world.

I want to share with you three practical steps you can take to begin the process of taking off your masks:

1. **Pour your heart out in prayer.** In your conversation with God, be real about your feelings and what you are experiencing. God already knows, but He wants you to let go and trust Him with all that concerns you. If you read any chapter in the book of Psalms, what you will find is that all of the authors literally poured their hearts out to God and ended with praise, as they trusted Him to work out their circumstances. We have to do the same. Pour your heart out to and trust God.

2. **Pour your heart out to a confidant.** Talk with someone whom you trust completely, someone who will be a sounding board for you, like a prayer partner. It is vital that we have at least one person to whom we can just pour out our hearts without shame or fear of judgment. I stress that this person should be a trusted confidant who will not gossip or share your business with others. If you have deep emotional issues or baggage, then seek a counselor for help. There isn't any shame in needing help, but there is shame in resisting it.

Perhaps you don't feel comfortable talking to someone else. If this is so, then follow step three.

3. **Pour your heart out in a journal.** Writing in a journal is a great way to release your feelings without sharing with another person. It's a good place to start if you are not ready to open up. Writing in a journal can help you sort through

some of your emotions. It will provide you with the ability to reflect back on what you are currently experiencing. I use journaling as a way to record my prayers and conversations with God. Many times, as I read back over my entries, I am reminded of how God has answered my prayers or changed my heart.

No matter what type of storm you are experiencing, deal with the issues that hinder you from living the abundant life that Jesus gives to all who believe in Him. Start trusting Him today so that you may accept yourself right where you are and experience peace beyond all understanding, no matter what life is throwing your way.

What mask are you wearing? Is it time to take it off?

Prayer

Lord, please help me to come to Your throne just as I am. You know the burdens that I carry, and You know the hurts that I hide in my heart. I will be honest with You: I cannot see my way through this storm. I am trying to hold it together and keep moving, but I am weary, Lord, and overwhelmed. Please give me the strength that I need to carry on. Thank You for the fact that I can lay my burdens at Your feet and receive Your promise of rest and peace. Thank You for walking with me through this storm and carrying me when needed. I know that I have victory in You. In Jesus' name, I pray. Amen.

Meditation Song

Meditate on the lyrics to the song "Walk by Faith" by Jeremy Camp.

Lesson 20

We Can Never Forget
Who God Is

"I am the Alpha and the Omega," says
the Lord God, "who is, and who was and
who is to come, the Almighty."
(Revelation 1:8 NIV)

This is an important lesson to remember at all times, but especially when you are in the storms of life. All of the previous nineteen lessons are important; however, this one trumps them all.

Remembering who God is allows you to trust Him and wait patiently on Him to act on your behalf. When you remember who He is, you know that there isn't a time, as His child, that He has ever left you alone. You know beyond a shadow of doubt that He can do anything but fail. And when He seems not to be acting on your behalf, trust me, He is moving behind the scenes to fulfill His perfect will for you.

When you become overwhelmed by the circumstances of your life and forget who God is, go deeper into His Word to help remind yourself. Go to your favorite Scriptures, or look at how He provided for countless others before you:

- God blessed Abraham and Sarah with a baby at their ripe ages of ninety.
- God restored Job, who experienced one devastation after another.
- God protected Daniel in the lions' den.
- God orchestrated Joseph's life to bless his family even after they betrayed him.
- God strategically placed Esther in the king's palace "for such a time as this" (Esther 4:14).

The greatest provision of them all is God's placing His only begotten Son in the womb of a virgin named Mary so that whosoever believes in Him shall live and have everlasting life. And if that wasn't enough, God's Son walked this earth to die a gruesome death. But thank God that that is not the end of the story, for the Bible tells us that Christ rose from the dead, conquering death and condemning the Enemy once and for all.

God did all of this for us—that we may live and weather the storms of life until He calls us home to glory.

My friend, if you don't remember anything else when you close this book, remember this one thing: God is God, no matter where you find yourself, and He loves you too much to ever leave you alone, for He has loved you with an everlasting love (Jeremiah 31:3). And that is one lesson you cannot afford ever to forget.

Prayer

Father God, thank You for revealing Yourself to me in this storm. You are awesome, and there is none like You. Your track record proves that You can do anything but fail. Your track record proves Your love for me over and over again. Thank You for who You are. Thank You for allowing me to have an intimate walk with You. Thank You for Your promises, Your provision, and Your protection. You are my lifeline, and I can never forget who You are. In Jesus' name, I pray. Amen.

Meditation Song

Meditate on the lyrics to the song "Yahweh" by Mali Music.

Lesson 21

Storms Teach Us to
Depend on God's Word

Your word is a lamp unto my feet
and a light unto my path.
(Psalm 119:105 NIV)

One day, I persisted in asking God, "Where am I, and how did I get here? And where am I in relation to where You are? Did I drift away unknowingly? How did I get all the way over here?"

The Holy Spirit simply said in reply, "You are right in the center of God's will for you."

Just because I have found myself in a storm does not mean that God has stopped being God and that He has somehow fallen off His throne. Just because I am experiencing stormy weather doesn't mean that I am outside of His will and that I somehow drifted in the wrong direction. For "He knows the plans that He has for me" (Jeremiah 29:11), and apparently I am right on track with His will for my life.

My friend Michael felt the need to remind me of this profound truth. While I was crying to him on the phone, he said that the Bible gives us prescriptions or remedies for how to deal with adversity. He said that there is nothing new under the sun and that I needed to rely only on what God reveals to me in His Word. He went on to say that my problem may not go away but that I would find comfort in God's Word.

I was grateful for the reminder.

In the dark, low moments, when you cannot feel the presence or the love of Jesus around you, you must remember that faith is not based on your feelings. When you feel as if you can no longer hold onto God, know that He is there holding onto you. Dark moments can overwhelm the best of us, as stormy weather threatens to shake our foundation.

When we feel all alone and find ourselves on the floor crying out, Satan comes and pounces on us; in those moments, all of his lies start to sound like the truth. During those times, we have to ignore our feelings and believe in God anyway. During those moments, we have to pull the Word of God out of our hearts and memory banks and just believe in every Scripture we have ever memorized.

We have to go into battle armed with the sword. We must speak against those feelings and say the following things in our strongest voice:

- "The Lord is my Shepherd; I shall not be in want" (Psalm 23:1).
- "God is my refuge and strength, a very present help in trouble" (Psalm 46:1).
- "The Lord will never leave me, nor forsake me" (Hebrews 13:5).
- "The Lord loves me with an everlasting love" (Jeremiah 31:3).
- "Greater is He that is within me than he that is in the world" (1 John 4:4).
- "The battle is not mine but the Lord's" (2 Chronicles 20:15b).
- "Our weapons are not carnal but mighty in pulling down strongholds" (2 Corinthians 10:3–4 KJV).

- "No weapon formed against me shall prosper" (Isaiah 54:17 NKJV).
- "I am the head and not the tail" (Deuteronomy 28:13).
- "The good works that God has started in me shall be completed" (Philippians 1:6).
- "I will trust God at all times" (Psalm 62:8).

When you have hit your lowest point and tell God that you can't bear anymore, that you can't hold on any longer, that is when the healing begins. For, in our weakness, His strength is perfect (2 Corinthians 12:9) and He is holding onto us. It reminds me of "Footprints in the Sand." God carries us when we can't carry on.

Prayer

Lord, I depend on You and You alone. I cannot continue to fight this battle with my own strength. I come to You, surrendering all. I know that You are bigger than anything I face in this world. I stand firmly on Your Word, which I have hidden in my heart. I stand firmly on Your promises. I trust in You. Move me out of the way, Lord, and have Your way. In the perfect name of Jesus, I pray. Amen.

Meditation Song

Meditate on the lyrics to the song "I Believe" by John P. Kee.

Lesson 22

Storms Help Us to See Things God's Way

And we know that all things work together
for good to them that love God, to them who
are called according to His purpose.
(Romans 8:28 KJV)

Here are three short words for you to ponder: *all, good,* and *His*.

These three short words pack a mighty punch, especially when one is living through a storm.

The first of the three words, *all,* literally means everything, the whole. You get it—leaving nothing out. God is working out the details of our lives in not some, but all, of the situations that we call good—and also those we call bad. Let us not forget that He is all-seeing, all-knowing, and all-powerful. Nothing catches Him off guard or throws His plan off.

The second word is *good*. This is a word that we mess up on because we don't necessarily always agree with what God calls good. In God's almighty dictionary, the word *good* does not include a mention of keeping us comfortable or even happy. Rather, in God's eyes, *good* means that no matter what happens in life, His grace is sufficient (2 Corinthians 12:9).

Good does not mean that everything works out as you would like it or even in your favor. It does not mean living without experiencing heartache, disappointment, or pain. It does not mean that life won't hurt, that you will not lose your job, that your spouse won't die or walk out on you. It doesn't mean that you will always have money in your bank or that you will have all that you dream of and more.

It doesn't mean any of that. In fact, those are the things that someone driving on autopilot would think. Those of us driven by the Holy Spirit understand that God defines the word *good* entirely differently. Remember, God is sovereign. He sees the beginning and the end and every little piece in between. Everything, big or small, has meaning and is working together for His good and perfect will.

Let's also remember that God gave His only Son Jesus to die on the cross. Jesus died a horrific, gruesome death, and God thought that that was good. I am forever grateful that He did. There is a wonderful song called "Blessings" by Laura Story that gives a whole different meaning to what blessings are and shows how *good* is redefined by God. After listening to this song, I realized that I, too, needed to redefine the word *good*.

The final word is *His*. Our lives are orchestrated to fulfill His purposes—not mine or yours, but *His*. We may not like His purpose, His ways, or His will, but He is trustworthy. We can rest in His arms, knowing that all of His ways are perfect and loving.

There is a Scripture in Isaiah 54:16–17 that helps put this idea in perspective. Basically, God said that He made the blacksmith and the coal that the blacksmith uses. But guess what? God then said that no weapon formed against you shall prosper. In other words,

God made all weapons, and not one of them can touch you or me without God's first granting His permission for them to be used in His good and perfect plan.

So, whatever storm you are experiencing, whatever pain keeps you up at night, understand that God is allowing it and will never give you more than you can bear. He promises that He will be there with you through it all. He says, "My grace is sufficient." And when you are weak, He becomes your strength (2 Corinthians 12:9).

Prayer

Lord, I will admit that, at times, I have had difficulty seeing things Your way and accepting Your will as best. I am learning to let go and just trust and rest in You. I am forever grateful that You saw it as good to sacrifice Your life so that we may have eternal life. I know that You give and take away, and that it is all according to Your good and perfect plan. Teach me to walk close to You and to trust in Your way, even when I don't understand. In your perfect name, I pray. Amen.

Meditation Song

Meditate on the lyrics to the song "How Great Is Our God" by LaRue Howard.

Lesson 23

Storms Don't Keep Us from God

> I can never escape from your spirit! I can
> never get away from your presence!
> (Psalm 139:7 NLT)

There is a saying that your best friend is the one who knows all about you yet still loves you. *God is that friend.*

When I read Psalm 139, I keep saying to myself, "Yet, God still loves me." He continues to pour out His love on us in spite of our sins, faults, and shortcomings. He knows everything, and yet He still loves us.

Take comfort in knowing that the amazing God who created heaven and earth knows you better than you know yourself. And because He knows you so well, this current storm you are in will not overtake you, will not overcome you. A God who knows just how much you can bear allowed it to happen. God also knows what it will take to mold you into His image. He knows your very core, and He knows what kind of storm will speak directly to where you are at this moment.

According to Psalm 139:7, the storm you are in has not removed you from the presence of God, for there is nowhere you can go that

God is not. He is omnipresent, and He promises never to leave us or forsake us (Deuteronomy 31:6). So, in the midnight hour when you feel alone, abandoned, and lost, remember that God is there and that His right hand will hold you and guide you through this dark moment (Psalm 139:10).

Even though a mother can lose her child in a busy shopping mall, God will never lose any of His children. He knows where we are at all times. This storm does not mean that He has fallen off His throne or that has He lost sight of us. He knows what we are going through every moment of every day that He blesses us with. Recall, as stated in the previous section, that He sticks closer than a brother. He is right there with us in the midst of this storm.

My best friend, Marcie, has been in a storm for nine years. When her daughter was three, she developed a life-threatening condition called Stevens–Johnson syndrome. It was the most difficult time of her life. While God spared her daughter's life, the time did not come without ongoing daily challenges. And through it all, Marcie has remained firm in her faith in God. Her unwavering faith has been an encouragement to me (and countless others) through my own health challenges. One day while encouraging me, she said, "At the end of the day, God has shown me what He can do, and I am not going to fall apart with every difficult situation." She went on to say, "In life, we can either turn to God or move farther away from Him. My choice is to turn to Him." Her storm did not keep her from God; it drew her closer.

Where are you right now? Are you able to say that you are drawing closer to God, or are you pushing away from Him because you find yourself in a difficult situation? My prayer is that you are allowing God to pull you closer to Him. My hope is that you are not leaning on your own understanding, but that you are trusting in the Lord.

During your storm, take the time to get to know God and to learn the promises and provisions He has just for you. God's character and His Word testify to His love and faithfulness to His children, which makes Him completely trustworthy, even when we don't understand or agree with His ways.

Prayer

Heavenly Father, through the power of the Holy Spirit living within me, I choose to turn to You in this storm. I choose to draw closer to You. I believe in Your Word, that all the days of my life were laid out before a single day had passed (Psalm 139:16b). You in Your sovereignty knew this moment would come, and You have given me all that I need to deal with it. I choose to lean on You and not on my own understanding (Proverbs 3:5b). I will not allow this storm to come between me and You; You are my lifeline and my hope. In Jesus' name, I pray. Amen.

Meditation Song

Meditate on the lyrics to the song "Seasons" by Donald Lawrence.

Lesson 24

Storms Remind Us of Past Blessings

I recall all you have done, O Lord; I remember
your wonderful deeds of long ago.
(Psalm 77:11 NLT)

What is the source of our distress in the midst of this storm?

The first answer we might give would likely be to name whatever is causing our storm. However, if we give more thought to the question, then we might find that our distress isn't really the storm, but our doubt that God will not provide for our needs, and our fear that He has abandoned us. It is not the storm in which we find ourselves that is the problem. It is actually our response to the storm. This, by far, has been the greatest lesson for me.

There is hope always in God's Word. I found this hope while thirsting for God's presence. I stumbled on Psalm 77 on my way to another passage, and I am glad that I did. Asaph, believed to be the writer of this psalm, was distressed over his doubt about God. He cried out questions that we all have when we are distressed, questions that even the faithful, seasoned believer asks: Has God forgotten? Has He withdrawn His love from me? Where is God?

Does He not hear my cry? Can He not feel my pain? Does He not see me?

Oh, but He does! We just have to remember all that He has done for us, even when we are in the midst of stormy weather. We have to remember what He has done all the days of our lives. Then, we have to praise Him for all those moments, remembering past blessings and the previous storms He brought us through. You have to recall how you praised Him then and allow that to carry you through this moment, too. We cannot afford to forget what God has already done.

In this passage, Asaph remembers what God did for him personally and what He did for the Israelites when they were led through the Red Sea by Moses and Aaron. We can find ourselves being modern-day Israelites, doubting what God can do. When I read this passage to my friend Michael, he said, "Man has not changed, but, thankfully, neither has God." God parts our Red Seas just like He did for the Israelites.

God takes care of His own in the good and in the bad. Remember: To our sovereign God, it is all good. We must turn our focus away from our problems and turn to God, the Creator of heaven and earth. He ordains every day of our lives, and we must praise Him for what He has already done!

Remember the blessings in the storm!

Prayer

Almighty God, You are always providing for me. Your blessings are all around me, every moment of every day. Please forgive me, for, at times, I forget what You have done. Lord, thank You for Your patience in dealing with me. Thank You for Your grace and mercy. I remember from where You have brought me, and I recall how You made a way when there seemed no way, time and time again. You hear my cry, and You see my tears. I trust that You will continue to part the "Red Seas" of my life and give me victory in this storm. In Jesus' name, I pray. Amen.

Meditation Song

Meditate on the lyrics to the song "You Are God Alone" by Phillips, Craig, and Dean.

Lesson 25

In the Storm, Do Not Lose Heart

We are hard pressed on every side, but not crushed;
perplexed, but not in despair; persecuted, but not
abandoned; struck down, but not destroyed.
(2 Corinthians 4:8–9 NIV)

Therefore we do not lose heart. Though
outwardly we are wasting away, yet inwardly
we are being renewed day by day. For our light
and momentary troubles are achieving for us an
eternal glory that far outweighs them all.
(2 Corinthians 4:16–18 NIV)

In the storms of life, it is easy to become distracted by the pain that
invades our world. Rather than focus on the pain, we have to focus
on God. In the end, our final objective is to be closer to God. It
may be hard to digest this while in the thick of it, but the storm
will not overtake us. Yes, it is difficult, but we must take comfort in
this passage. We are not crushed, we are not in despair, and we are
not abandoned—nor are we destroyed. Because of God's everlasting
love, we do not lose hope. Our inner strength is being renewed
every day. And it is in our weaknesses that God's strength is perfect
(2 Corinthians 12:9).

During this storm, follow the words of 2 Corinthians 4:16: "Do not lose heart." In other words, do not allow your problems to become bigger than God or stronger than your faith in God, who raised Jesus from the dead. Trust in Him even more, understanding that there is a divine purpose for this storm. We may not understand it, but we walk by faith and not by the heartache and devastation that we see all around us. We cling to God's promises, and we fix our eyes on Jesus. We fix our eyes on the hope that better days are ahead.

One day, my friend Alison told me that we shouldn't take everything personally. She suggested the acronym QTIP—"quit taking it personal." In other words, sometimes the storms of life aren't about you, but all about God and His greater purpose being fulfilled through you. Verse 17 of the above passage confirms that our momentary troubles are achieving for us an eternal glory that far outweighs what we are experiencing.

And this is why praising God in the midst of the storm is vital. Praise allows us to direct our focus away from our problems and focus instead on God and His promises. When we do this, we realize that God is bigger than any problem we face. We realize that we are in the arms of a mighty God, one who can do anything but fail.

No matter the duration or intensity of the storm, do not lose heart. Do not give up. Do not get distracted by all that is wrong at this moment. You must, by all means necessary, continue to trust in God. You must, above all, stand firmly on His promises. When you find yourself at the end of the rope or you think that you have reached the limit of all that you can bear, revisit these passages and remember that because of God, we cannot lose hope. Hang on. There are blessings falling all around you.

Prayer

Lord Jesus, You are mighty to save, and You are mighty to do great things. I will trust You, and I will not lose heart. Holy Spirit, please help me to keep moving forward, with my eyes fixed on Jesus. Holy Spirit, when I am weak and discouraged, encourage my spirit and give me the strength to hold on. I can only weather this storm through Your power. In Jesus' name, I pray and claim victory over this storm. Amen.

Meditation Song

Meditate on the lyrics to the song "Mighty to Save" performed by Anthony Evans.

One Last Thought

Be my rock of refuge, to which I can
always go; give the command to save me,
for you are my rock and my fortress.
(Psalm 71:3 NIV)

If God wanted to end the storm, all He would have to do is give the command and it would be gone. It would become a faint memory. But there must be something else we need, something else we need to learn about Him, about ourselves, and about life.

One thing I have learned for sure is that His grace is sufficient and that joy really does come in the morning. No matter how uncomfortable the pain has been, I open my eyes each day and see new mercies. Even though the pain remains, God shows me, through His grace and mercy, how to embrace it, welcome it, and learn from it. To some, this may sound like I am one of those who like pain. That is far from the truth. Instead, I am choosing to embrace what I cannot control and to learn from it rather than fight it.

One of my favorite passages is Psalm 9:9: "The Lord also will be a refuge for the oppressed, a refuge in times of trouble." *The Life Application Study Bible* says the following about this verse: "God's promise does not mean that if we trust in Him, we will escape loss or suffering; it means that God Himself will never leave us, no matter what we face."[6]

No matter what storm we find ourselves in at any moment, God is with us. When we seek Him, we find that He sticks closer than a brother. It reminds me of the story of the footprints in the sand. During our darkest moments, God is not only there with us but is also carrying us.

That is the kind of God we serve!

And God can handle anything, everything, all things that we experience in life. But we have to trust Him and move out of the way to let Him have His way. The storms of life can make us bitter if we don't surrender ourselves to God. The storms can be very powerful, and they have the potential of doing more harm than good. Their outcome depends on our response to them.

One day while my brother was visiting, he told me that he wasn't too worried about me because, as he said, "God's got you, and you will be okay." And he was right. God does have me. Even though I struggle during this challenging (to say the least) moment in my life, God has proven over and over again that He knows what He is doing.

Several months later, I find myself still in the storm, with no end in sight. Yet, through it all, I was pleased to hear my mom say that I had weathered this storm like a champ. She said, "Your faith is stronger than ever." Though the winds blow and the heavy rain falls, my roots have grown deeper. I am clinging to God even more. I wonder if this would be true if I had not been thrown into this storm. Would this be true if my faith had not been tested? I am not sure. But I do know that when we come face-to-face with adversity, we really do get to know God.

The lessons I have learned are invaluable, and I could not have learned them without this storm. I am grateful that God knows best and that He is always behind the scenes working life out according to

His good and perfect plan. And in the end, what the Enemy meant for bad, God used for good.

God bless you.

Appendix

These Bible verses are for you to recite when you are in the midst of a battle of the mind. We cannot afford to forget that the Enemy prowls around like a lion, looking for the one he can devour, destroy, and kill (1 Peter 5:8). When you are in the midst of a storm, you are the target that he is after. The only weapon you have to defeat the Enemy is Scripture.

These verses helped me to defeat the Enemy many nights. It is true that once you have fought the battle, joy really comes in the morning.

Habakkuk 3:18   "Yet I will rejoice in the Lord, I will be joyful in God my savior." NIV

Psalm 25:10a   "All the ways of the Lord are loving and faithful." NIV

Psalm 30:5b   "Joy comes in the morning." NASB

Psalm 29:10a   "The Lord sits enthroned over the flood." NIV

Psalm 33:20–22 "We wait in hope for the Lord; he is our help and our shield." NIV

Isaiah 54:17   "No weapon that is formed against you shall prosper." NASB

Acknowledgments

This book would not have come to fruition without the encouragement, support, and guidance of so many people. My heart is overflowing with gratitude and deep appreciation. I am blessed by your presence in my life. You know who you are, and you are forever engraved in my heart and in my prayers.

Special acknowledgement to Kathy Chambers and Lila Mills for all of your hard work helping to shape the original manuscript.

About the Author

Natalie Brown Rudd is an associate minister at Antioch Baptist Church in Cleveland, Ohio, where she serves in the women's ministry as a small-group Bible study leader. She is a student at Ashland Theological Seminary and is the founder of Because of His Grace Ministries, which influence the spiritual growth of women. She is a sought-after speaker and teacher at churches, conferences,  seminars, and Women's Day services. Natalie is available for speaking engagements and may be contacted through her website at www. becauseofhisgrace.com.

Sources

Lesson Two: Storms Are Holy Ground
1   Stanley, Charles. "Seeing Adversity from God's Viewpoint." *InTouch Magazine* (July 11, 2012): 43.

Lesson Three: Storms Change Your Focus
2   Wesemann, Tim, ed. *Facing Illness with Hope.*, 31.

Lesson Four: Storms Are for a Far Greater Purpose
3   Schutte, Shana. "Doubt: A Catalyst to Faith." *Just Between Us* (2012): 12.

Lesson Eleven: It Really Is Okay to Cry with Someone
4   Brett, Regina. *God Never Blinks.*, 35.

Lesson Twelve: Storms Are Invitations, Not Interruptions
5   Gieschen, Erin. "Invisible Heroics." *InTouch Magazine* (August 2012): 33.

One Last Thought
6   *The Life Application Study Bible, New International Version,* published by Tyndale House Publishers, Inc., and Zondervan Publishing House. Copyright © 1995 by Tyndale House Publishers, Inc., Wheaton, IL.